T0285335

Ordinary Disasters

Ordinary Disasters

How I Stopped Being a Model Minority

Anne Anlin Cheng

Pantheon Books
New York

All rights reserved. Published in the United States by Pantheon Books,
a division of Penguin Random House LLC, New York, and distributed
in Canada by Penguin Random House Canada Limited, Toronto.

Pantheon Books and colophon are registered trademarks
of Penguin Random House LLC.

Several pieces, and excerpts, first appeared in different form in *The
Atlantic, Hyperallergic, The Nation, The New York Times, Periodical
for the Modern Language Association,* and *The Washington Post.*

Grateful acknowledgment is made to Alfred Music for permission
to reprint lyrics from "Looking at You" (from *Wake Up and Dream*).
Words and music by Cole Porter. © 1929 (Renewed) WC Music
Corp. All rights reserved. Used by permission of Alfred Music.

Publication is made possible in part by a grant from the Barr Ferree Foundation
Publication Fund, Department of Art and Archaeology, Princeton University.

Library of Congress Cataloging-in-Publication Data
Names: Cheng, Anne Anlin, author.
Title: Ordinary disasters : how I stopped being a model minority / Anne Anlin Cheng.
Description: First edition. | New York : Pantheon Books, [2024] |
Includes bibliographical references.
Identifiers: LCCN 2023055096 (print) | LCCN 2023055097 (ebook) |
ISBN 9780593316825 (hardcover) | ISBN 9780593316832 (ebook)
Subjects: LCSH: Cheng, Anne Anlin. | Cheng, Anne Anlin—Family. | Taiwanese
Americans—Biography. | Cancer—Patients—United States—Biography. | Feminine
beauty (Aesthetics) | Asian Americans—Social conditions. | United States—Race
relations—Psychological aspects. Classification: LCC E184.T35 C476 2024 (print)
| LCC E184.T35 (ebook) | DDC 973.0495/073092 [B]—dc23/eng/20231229
LC record available at https://lccn.loc.gov/2023055096
LC ebook record available at https://lccn.loc.gov/2023055097

www.pantheonbooks.com

Spine artwork: *Fly,* 2007, ink on flax paper, by Peng Wei
Jacket design by Linda Huang

Printed in the United States of America
First Edition
2 4 6 8 9 7 5 3 1

For my loved ones
& all those who came before

Contents

Preface

I was going through cancer when the world got sick: a raging pandemic and unabashed racism sweeping our country even as I sheltered at home, struggling with the shell of my body. All my usual resources—my intellectual work, my personal faith in justice and self-determinism, my sense of self-mastery—crashed around me, inadequate to the forces hitting me.

These essays are a way back to myself, or, more accurately, to arrive at a self that I have yet to fully own.

It took a series of crises both private and global—from that early Saturday-morning phone call that shattered my world to the subsequent sidewise tilt of the world outside—to make me realize I had been living a life half hidden. There has been so much lost and unsaid between the constant navigation of multiple worlds and the many filters that both enabled and shielded me. I started to see that I had been busy living a free life without really being a free person.

I've been a scholar of race and gender for more than three decades. I still find it hard to say certain truths. There is a world of difference between *knowing* and *living*. And sometimes knowing can occlude living.

I want to face and work through these essays a series of personal, idiosyncratic encounters: ordinary disasters that gave me heartache but went silently by. These seemingly small moments bear the invisible imprints of larger social and cultural forces: the uneven yet intense collisions of racialization, gender expectations, immigration, multiple layers of colonialism embedded in the histories of East-and-West impacting an individual life. But these larger systems of power and desire have also failed to wholly define, even as they shaped, my most intimate loves.

Anne Carson says that candor is like "a skein being produced inside the belly day after day, it has to get itself woven out somewhere." Terry Tempest Williams says that silence is "the unnatural thwarting of what struggles, to come into being, but cannot." For me, it's more like carrying inside me, alongside the tumors, a series of tight knots, some red and pulsing like mini hearts, some mute and burrowed.

These essays attempt to pull at these knots, strands of what it means to be an immigrant, to become Asian American, to form an interracial couple in a time of multiple disasters. They give voice to the shredding attachments of mothers and daughters; how the past rises to meet us when we are facing the other way; how we can lose a whole world without fanfare; how racial grief and private griefs cloak one another; how we ghost ourselves from our loved ones; and the nature of beauty for the unbeautiful. They are intensely personal, these knots, and some can never be fully untied. But sometimes, in the face of life's irresolvable paradoxes, it is enough just to be able to acknowledge the contradictions under which one lives. Sometimes, finding acts of beauty in a broken world means being able to take stock of yourself—to write out the tangles—among the wreckage.

I can no longer take my future days for granted. Writing offers me a dwelling when I feel the most homeless. These essays are, in their way, letters to loved ones, those who are no longer here and cannot listen, and those present but too close to speak to. They are also letters to myself.

Intimacy

Part 1

The Monk and the Soldier

When I shaved my head in anticipation of chemotherapy, two things happened. First, just like that, I stopped looking like a woman. Second, I turned into a monk. My husband, peering in the mirror, said, "Hey, you look like a cute monk!" I am pretty sure the "cute" part came out of love, but the "monk" part, echoing my thoughts, struck me as a notable coincidence. In the spirit of camaraderie, he, too, shaved his head. But he did not look less male, nor did he look like a monk. Being tall and white, he looked, well, military. So there we were: the monk and the soldier.

Given how complex gender and race are as embodied experiences, it is remarkable how simplistic and crude their visual expressions are. Could hair, a minor loss in the violence of cancer, make such a great difference? I knew, at least intellectually, that "woman" has always been reducible to her body parts, but to see such an insight so viscerally and mundanely demonstrated in the bathroom mirror stunned me. And what was with the monk? Would my husband have thought I looked like a monk had he not grown up watching kung fu movies? Would I, had

I not immigrated to the United States? Have I come to see my own Chineseness through Western tropes?

In the 1990s, when I lived in Northern California, the *San Francisco Bay Guardian* ran an article about the great number of relationships between Asian women and white men. The article quoted an undergraduate from the University of California, Berkeley, who, asked why she preferred dating white men over Asians, said, "Well, it kind of feels incestuous to me . . . like dating my brother." A friend who read the article poked fun at this admission, saying, "Good thing people in Asia don't think so!" But there's something behind what that young woman said— a thin line of grief or maybe of querulousness, an expression of familial allergy—that has stayed with me.

Scholars have long pointed to the hypersexualization of Asian women and the demasculinization of Asian men in American popular media as a leading cause for the high rate of Asian American women marrying outside their race. But it is also common wisdom among Asian American women of my generation and younger that, if you discover your white boyfriend has been exclusively dating Asian women, you should run for the hills. Just because there is a white-male fetishization of Asian femininity does not mean that the inverse (that is, Asian-female fetishization or idealization of white masculinity) is true. In fact, for many Asian women involved in interracial relationships, myself included, white masculinity is a fraught challenge. Racialized gender, especially as it plays out in intimate relationships, is not and cannot be simply a question of identity politics or a problem of representation.

The young woman's confession in that interview seems to me

to speak more to a deeper and more silent dilemma of intimacy for the diasporic subject, a wound in the experience of kinship itself. Kinship, after all, is about determining who is a stranger and who is not. It is generally agreed, certainly in Western cultures, that the social norm of marrying outside one's community, clan, or tribe produces biological, economic, and cultural advantages. (Anthropologists call this *exogamy*.) The injunction to marry outside one's bloodline to ensure genetic diversity and create social alliances, however, takes on different and confusing meanings when your clan or community has been truncated or displaced, at once insular and under assault.

For many immigrant communities, marriage within one's ethnic group (*endogamy*) ensures cultural and familial continuity in the face of fragmenting, geographic dispersal. Here, then, is the double bind for the racialized minority: marrying out means selling out, while marrying in can feel like giving in to conservative familial demands on the one hand and xenophobic prohibition on the other. Only within the peculiarities of American racial dynamics can traditional, racist white anxiety about miscegenation find a ready ally with traditional Asian family values. Both sides apply patriarchal and racial restrictions within which the Asian American woman must navigate.

Love can be challenging. Add being Asian and a woman in America, and you get a vexing picture. As Cathy Park Hong sums it up in *Minor Feelings,* "In the popular imagination, Asian Americans inhabit a vague purgatorial status . . . distrusted by African Americans, ignored by whites, unless we're being used by whites to keep the black man down." Used as pawns in the game of racial divisiveness, Asian Americans are often despised for their reputed adjacency to whiteness and economic privileges. In a 2012 study, the psychologist Susan Fiske showed that most Americans rate Asians and Asian Americans as highly "competent" or "intelligent," but almost all found the latter to be "cold" or "not warm"—that is, unloved and unlovable. The result is not surprising, especially since the very terms of the survey ("competence" and "likability") already scripted the yardstick against which Asianness gets judged.

The Asian American woman would seem to fare better than her male counterpart on the likability scale. She at least can claim access to the idea of erotic or exotic appeal. But this privilege also spells her downfall. At once the lotus blossom and the dragon lady, the celestial being and the pestilential prostitute (according to nineteenth-century immigration laws), Asian beauty in America is, historically and now, an ugly business. To this day, the Asian American woman occupies a weird place in the American racial imaginary: she has absorbed centuries of the most blatant racist and sexist projections, yet she hardly registers in the public consciousness as a minority, much less a figure who has suffered discrimination.

The writer David Xu Borgonjon once wryly observed, "You can only be Asian outside of Asia." For the Asian American woman, I would add, she can be neither wholly Asian nor wholly American. Seen as both a prize and a liability, she is caught between sets of double elimination that make the question of love—and the stranger-versus-family distinction—confounding, even perilous.

Years ago, when my husband was out shopping with our newborn, a woman in the store approached him and asked eagerly, "I got my daughter from China. Where did you get yours?" My husband was amused by the encounter, but I recall being pained. Did my husband, even for a second, feel that our daughter was foreign to him? Did the incident jar him out of the cocoon of our new family? I also remember not being able to bring myself to ask these questions out loud.

My husband and I had taken on so many challenges beyond becoming an interracial couple: getting married as older adults; learning to meld two full, separate, and idiosyncratic lives; buying a house we could barely afford; confronting parenthood for the first time. So why was I unsettled by a stranger's perception?

That's the power of the third gaze. I can dismiss the woman's clumsy assumption, itself most likely driven by a longing for community, but her misrecognition is not unlike what haunts my extended family. Members of my side of the family invariably remark how white my children look, while my husband's side observes how Chinese they look. There's what the world out there sees, and then there's our lived, affective reality. The two are not the same, but they are not wholly disconnected from each other, either.

Familiarity and intimacy are in fact strange, complex, and fragile conditions of being—at once magically capable of being forged and terribly easy to rupture. Sometimes the dance of strangeness and familiarity in my marriage (those tiny shifts of reality) baffles me, the ways in which quotidian intimacy can energize or hinder our togetherness. We come in and out of focus in everyday living. The more familiar we are with each other, the more intimacy becomes both a lifeline and an obstacle, something we rely on but also something that foils us when we most need to see each other afresh. In minor, daily acts, like chatting over washing dishes, we swell in the luxury of shared rhythm and private language, but a particular turn of phrase or a tone that the other recognizes all too well can abruptly open a jagged breach. This, too, is difference at work.

In 1920, W. E. B. Du Bois wrote a haunting story called "The Comet," a dystopian vision of the end of the world in which, at long last, interracial love (between the last white woman and the last Black man on Earth) could be redeemed. Only with the apparent end of the world and the breakdown of all societal rules, according to Du Bois, can love between the races be imaginable. But in the story, it turns out that only their city was destroyed, her family returns in the end, and all that was between the lovers is dashed, erased as if it had never been. Do we need to face death or disaster to own interracial love or risk its ruptures?

My husband and I are such opposites. There are times when I feel the insurmountable wall of our differences—his stubbornness, his maleness, his whiteness. Yet I have also grown from his determination, his unshakable faith in our ability and right to thrive in this world. When cancer and chemo stripped me down to the core, there was no one else on Earth on whom the bare skeleton of me could lean other than him.

My husband's ease in the world is both who he is and the result of how he moves in the world. His presence in most spaces is rarely questioned. I enter a room and immediately scan it for Asians or other people of color, their number (whether none or many) calling for different social arsenals. Over the years, I have developed enough of a mask of composure to be highly functional. Few people know how much mental energy it takes for me to enter a room full of people or to talk to a stranger. A very old friend once observed that watching me at a dinner party was like watching a duck on a pond: above the water, smooth gliding; under the water, the frantic flutter of feet.

Family lore tells of a different child in Taiwan, one who talked back whenever she was told girls are disposable, one who wore a glaring yellow-and-orange bell-bottom suit to a uniformed school on picture day. That cocky girl disappeared around the time of our move to America. I think I lost her to immigration and puberty. Her departure was so gradual that it was not so much a loss as a forgetting. She disappeared behind little punctuating moments: Adrianne—pink, blond, green-eyed, and one of my first American friends—pinching my skin and exclaiming, "You are not yellow at all!"; my father telling me not to call him "Pop-pi" anymore because in America it sounded as if I were calling a puppy; the only other Asian American girl in my high school snubbing me because people assumed we would be friends.

It took years for me to acknowledge my deep sense of unbelonging in America. Such admission would feel like a great failure. It would mean I have fallen into the petty trap of the disgruntled other, like the child who, in demanding to know why she was not invited to a party, exposes her longing. Or it would mean I have not worked hard enough or have not been good enough to master my limitations. To this day, I fluctuate between trying to own categories I occupy and trying to resist those that own me. Recently, after working on a yearlong committee with a group of colleagues, I overheard one of them say, "And we even had a Chinese woman on the committee with us." What feels so terrible about social alienation is that it can divide you from yourself.

—

Even as I grow older and kinder to myself, my body seems intent on repeating the habit of dis-ease. First came the day I lost; they call it transient global amnesia. (Wasn't I, an immigrant transplanted from Taipei to Augusta, Georgia, and who had for decades since bounced back and forth between New York and the San Francisco Bay Area, already a globally transient subject?) During those lost hours, my brain hiccupped like a broken toy; my reality restarted every ten minutes or so. I would have preferred to be out cold over that frightening, unreliable consciousness.

Then came a series of autoimmune issues. "It's as if your body thinks it is under constant threat, so it attacks itself," the doctors explained. Nothing quite like being told that your body is working against you—that is, until you are told there is actual malignancy in your body. When I woke up in the operating room after my cancer surgery, I could not speak but could hear loud noises, metal clanking, and people murmuring. Someone pulled something hard out of my throat, and my body told me hands were pulling and pushing parts of me that I could not really feel. In a moment of panic, I wondered if they knew I had woken up early.

There are many ways of being made a stranger to yourself. When the chemo began to leach my interiority, empty me out like a used bag, I took on a transparency and became a ghost behind glass, unreachable even to myself. In those nondays, the only anchor against my vanishing was my effort to approximate being a parent and a person.

All the words we have around cancer—militarized ones like *fighting* or euphemistic ones like *treatment*—really end up sealing an experience that is nearly impossible to describe, because it is all about merciless eradication at the very cellular level of your being, not pain as we know it but an awful erasure of your mind, your being, *you*. The truth was that I felt indifferent, unmoored from everything and everyone, even from the life I was laboring to save. My body sat on me like armor even as it refused sanctuary. When I could read again, I found these lines from the poet Jacqui Germain:

> My body is a haunted house that I am lost in.
> There are no doors but there are knives and a hundred
>   windows.

The tail end of my treatment coincided with the outbreak of the Covid-19 pandemic. My self-isolation blended into the world's quarantine. It was heart-sinking enough to confront my mortality; then, almost every week, I had to process news of the death of family members, friends, former teachers. We all know we are going to die one day, but the force of that knowledge can be felt only when death breaks into your path and sits on your chest.

Covid-19 has made it clear how interconnected we all are. It has shown that the question of life itself is not only a biological one but also an ethical one: Whose life counts? How do you take care of yourself and others? What is your responsibility to those who are the most vulnerable? Constraint and responsibility have always been conditions of, not exceptions to, freedom. Yet this shared proximity to disaster and the huge losses incurred have not been able to protect us from old enmities—the fact that we in 2020 still must argue for the value of Black lives, that attacks on people of Asian descent are on the rise.

I was wrong to think a shared global health crisis would save us from racial antagonism. It's the opposite: the viral crisis has become a vector for the racism that has always spoken in and circulated through the language of contamination. Anti-Black and anti-Asian sentiments are born from at least three centuries of American racial strife, the enduring, knotted legacy of systemic and cultural racism. They become only more vivified in the presence of other disasters.

More and more, I fear that Du Bois's vision remains prophetic; even the end of the world is not enough to warrant love between the races or make claims for a fundamental regard for life.

My husband and I did not come to be the monk and the soldier in this world accidentally. As I write, it occurs to me that, aside from the exotic Asian woman, the monk and the soldier might be two of the most iconic and loaded figures to emerge out of East-West entanglements. U.S. militarized presence in Asia for the better part of the twentieth century has made the soldier *the* representative American figure for many people outside the United States, while the monk has become for the West the very symbol of Asian passivity and outdatedness, whose extinction has been safeguarded against only by its occasional usefulness as an appropriable source of Eastern mysticism. Given the contemporary rhetoric of contagion (surrounding both disease and the immigrant) and the anti-Chinese xenophobia revived by the pandemic, the monk is hardly quarantined from the stigma that is as old as the "yellow peril" and as recent as the "China virus" or "kung flu," in the words of a former president.

That my husband and I, in the darkest moment of our private reckoning, in the face of a threat to our very future, should end up reproducing the flat outlines of these mirror images has everything to do with the racial and gender formulations that inevitably shape and fall terribly short of who we are. It tells us how powerful and yet also how impoverished cultural images are. How they move us and how we move through them can be at once coercive and unpredictable. There are days when my husband is my most cherished interlocutor, and there are days when I feel keenly that he will forever remain a stranger to the immigrant in me. Both are true and are the conditions of our intimacy and our separateness.

The monk and the soldier are not so different—both figures of discipline and endurance. The shadow of disaster (cancer, a global pandemic, racial violence) makes and unmakes them, just as my husband and I have had to readjust, moment to moment, our ideas of what constitutes survival, what kind of strength is needed to let go and what to hang on. *(Write it!)* I may live for several more years or a few more months. For the time I have, I want to live honestly. I want to stop proving my worth to a world that treats the diligent but tiresome Asian American woman with convenience and contempt.

It is crushing to be reduced to a cancer patient or the Asian wife of a white man or yet another woman of color. I feel like none of those things, yet I live the reality of all of those things. I want to shore up my energy and concentrate on things and relationships that give me meaning and joy. I would say I was going to Marie Kondo my relationships, except I'm troubled by how this lifestyle guru acquires her enormous popularity by drawing on old ideas of Asian femininity: the lingering myth of Eastern simplicity and restraint, the fantasized beauty of making yourself neat and small. It takes too much psychic effort to be always good and controlled, constantly self-curating, and vigilantly tuned into the minefield of multiple consciousness. I want to own a life to which I am directly connected.

Two months after my last treatment, my hair started to grow back. The dream was pixie chic, but the reality more resembled a lapsed monk. When the unruly fuzz started to appear, my husband and this time my son, too, shaved their hair so we could have a hair-growing contest. Every evening after dinner, at the same time and in the same spot in the house, we took a picture of our naked heads to document what had grown. We knew we were really tracking the imperceptible, running an unseen race. Death now forever moves through the center of our days. The little bubble of our family, so clearly drawn by the quarantine, holds its own slow time.

2

Striving

For most of my adult life, I've been a hard worker, reliable, and conscientious. I took my teaching seriously, and my research even more so. I assumed institutional service with commitment and good cheer. I was, in short, the model minority whom I deconstructed with my students in the classroom. But in the past several years, the veneer has started to crack.

At work, I had been embroiled in decades of institution building (aka, institutional fighting), struggling to establish a broader and more inclusive curriculum in race and ethnic studies—what I thought the institution wanted. But when I started to ask for real institutional changes, I found myself caught between a white administration whose reluctance could only be taken as indifference at best and racist at worst and a small cohort of beleaguered colleagues of color whose enforced and habituated territorialism put up roadblocks of their own. I was the institution's poster child for diversity, my labor its alibi, my perseverance praiseworthy but tiresome to others.

At home, my husband and I were not doing well. The smooth surface of our marriage showed fissures. Why was every conversation about politics shot through with tension?

Then one day at work in a department meeting for African American studies, where I had held a joint appointment as a comparative race scholar, a colleague whose work I respected a great deal said, "Black studies should only be taught by Black scholars." I looked around the room; no one said anything or met my gaze. Then the one white woman in the room nodded in eager consent. I wondered whether out of white guilt or overidentification she was assenting to her own disqualification from that table.

I was used to the perils of identity politics in academia, and I had always known that "optics" played a complicated role in African American studies departments across the country—indeed, in almost all the so-called identity fields—but I hadn't thought I would have to do versions of this battle here among other people of color. I didn't protest, feeling like it wasn't a battle I could win. I left the meeting devastated, feeling rejected by a field to which I had devoted so many years of labor and heart.

A permanent pain grew in my stomach. I started to wake at two a.m. regularly and could not go back to sleep. My husband scolded me for allowing other people's opinions to impact me so deeply. He did not understand why I took all the politics at work so personally. I could see the gulf stretching between us even as I could not identify the exact cause. It felt as if I was at war with everyone, including my partner and my own body.

Even before the cancer diagnosis, in those stressful years I found myself in and out of intensive care units for inexplicable, one-off traumatic episodes. At one point I fell into a miserable flu-like state that lasted for almost a year. I bounced from specialist to specialist. Antibiotics and steroids didn't help. I developed cyclical fevers. I lost my voice completely. I thought I was turning into the textbook hysteric and considered checking into the Mayo Clinic. I could hear the impatience edging my husband's concern. I was letting him and everyone else down. I wondered whether I had the energy to find an apartment and move out. I couldn't battle the institution at work, combat this mystery illness, and fight my husband's disappointment, too.

At a low point in our marriage, my husband said, "I don't know what has happened to you. You've become such an Eeyore." Could there be anything more painful than to be accused of failing to live up to the woman your husband married?

In hindsight, it was the worst thing he could have said to me back then: hitting my deep, unacknowledged fear that I would not be worthy without my sunny, hardworking self.

It felt as if I was going through two divorces, at work and at home.

When the diagnosis of Sjögren's syndrome finally emerged, I felt relieved, even though I had never heard of it and the word *chronic* didn't sound good. But at least it was something real. Sjögren's is one of those invisible diseases where the patients look fine, but inside their bodies are waging wars, generating systemic inflammation. It short-circuits the signals from the moisture-producing glands in your body, impacting the functions of your eyes, mouth, throat, lungs, and stomach. This is why Sjögren's patients need a "team" of attending specialists. I have since learned that Sjögren's affects as many as four million people in the United States. Doctors know very little about it. It remains one of the most un- or misdiagnosed diseases.

Ninety-nine percent of those who suffer from Sjögren's syndrome are women.

Oh, another peculiar symptom of Sjögren's: the inability to shed tears.

My hard-to-please father, who had wanted me to marry a Taiwanese surgeon, found himself taken by my new husband's Paul Bunyan–like spirit. One of the first sights my dad had of his future son-in-law (not a doctor but a Silicon Valley tech guy) was when the latter was on his hands and knees refinishing the wood floors of the fixer-upper into which we planned to move. My husband would go to the empty house at the end of the day and work on the house until well past midnight, using battery-powered floodlights once it got dark because the electricity had not yet been turned on.

We put ourselves in deep debt to purchase this tiny house in Burlingame, California, midpoint between his commute down the peninsula to Silicon Valley and my commute across the Bay Bridge to Berkeley, where I was teaching. After we moved in, we painted the house a pale lemon. He did most of the work, but I, pregnant with our first child by then, did my share, covering the lower half of the house while sitting on an upside-down bucket with my big belly. We called the house our little love bungalow. The house was more than seventy-five years old and barely a thousand square feet but had a well-centered floor plan. It boasted those no-longer-available, never-rotting, two-by-four redwood boards behind the drywall, but it also had a leaky foundation and the ugliest turquoise carpet I had ever seen. We had no money to hire people, so my husband did everything himself. He tore up the carpet, researched online the best way to finish wood floors, and proceeded to do so. He restored the roof, carrying hundreds of tons of shingles up and down the ladder for several days. And when he wanted to replace the old knob-and-tube electrical wiring in the house, he downloaded a one-hundred-page electrician manual, read it from start to finish (that, for me, was itself a feat), then proceeded to pull out all the old wires and put in a modern Romex system that the inspector praised.

"How very American!" my dad had said, shaking his head in amazement and admiration. I could hear in his voice an echo of that old idealism about American can-do.

I, too, had felt buoyed by my new spouse's fearlessness and resourcefulness. I was used to hard work myself, but not with such optimism. I had always anticipated the worst, vigilant against risks, and here came this person who believed anything was possible and would turn out well if you put your mind and energy to it. The area inside my chest cavity felt larger. We were in our late thirties but felt younger. Those early years were filled with sunshine and busyness, evening walks among the scents of jasmine and jacaranda, living from paycheck to paycheck, partnering on the joint project of baby cries and feedings, pacing in tandem. I remember thinking, *Wow, a life where love and belonging come naturally.*

Coming back to the East Coast reminded me of how race in America, for the most part, remains black and white. On the East Coast and in the world of the Ivy League, Asians rarely fall into the calculus, except when being invoked as a threat to Blacks and whites. The university to which I moved claimed that it was committed to building Asian American studies, but a dean had leaned in to ask conspiratorially, "So is there even such a thing as Asian American literature?" The university librarian kindly took me on a tour of the East Asian language stacks, while I gently informed him that although I do happen to read Mandarin, Asian American literature is largely written in English. I had to recalibrate my teaching, too. You cannot teach a critique of identity politics to an audience unaware of why we need identity politics in the first place.

The move also brought back memories of growing up in the South. As the first and only Asians in the Episcopal Day School in Augusta, Georgia, my brother and I were treated with more curiosity than hostility, though there was the time a boy from the back of the school bus yelled at me as I got on, "Go back to where you came from, or we'll bomb your Pearl Harbor!" I was a kid myself, and I was baffled. Didn't the U.S. own Pearl Harbor?

Looking back, I see that one problem over time was that my husband remained unshaken in his faith in self-reliance while I was hitting the walls of mine.

I'm not just talking about the "bamboo ceiling," though there's that, too. I'm referring to the realization that no matter how hard I worked or how much I mastered, I would never be able to exceed the flat outline of how I appear to the world: just another Chinese woman. What I imagined to be my will and self-determination—my individualism and my drive to work harder, learn more, do better, never settle for complacency, keep peace, be responsible, be likable—was in fact stoking the embers of my stereotype and my erasure. The eruption of anti-Asian hate and violence at the height of the pandemic showed the racist and xenophobic resentment the figure of the Asian has always incited in America. It didn't matter that Asian Americans largely appeared eager to assimilate; it didn't matter that Chinatowns across the U.S. had the lowest rates of Covid infection despite crowded quarters; Asian Americans were still seen as vectors of disease.

When I was growing up, my parents told my brother and me that we had to work three times as hard to get half as far as regular Americans, by which they meant white people. Yet words like *prejudice* and *discrimination* were never used in our household growing up; they were taboo, excuses for your own failings. Never compare yourself down. If you're at the top 1 percent, worry about others in that 1 percent.

The more assimilated you are, the less likely you will be dinged by prejudice. At least, that is the working myth. And the more you disavow the labor of that adjustment, the more you can believe in that myth. Like an invisible disease, assimilation is at its best when it's undetectable. The sociologist Erving Goffman calls assimilation "covering": the idea that you downplay or cover over your differences to match mainstream culture or expectation. Assimilation is not passing. It's more of a shell game.

The good assimilationist, like the good girl, puts on a good face, makes herself a little smaller for the ease of others, does whatever is necessary to sustain the smooth surface of sociality. It's not because things are easier when you give in or simply because you want to please; it's because what's on the other side of that civility is a violence so quotidian and profound that your very survival is at stake.

When I was walking on the towpath by the lake near my house and a cyclist rushed past me a little too close and a little too fast with a "Fucking Chinese tourist!" jettisoned at me, I was filled with impotent rage. Why didn't I yell back? I was equally restrained at the dinner party where another guest asked me if my daughter was biracial and when I replied yes, he said with a mixture of marvel and chagrin, "Gosh, those Chinese genes are so darn strong, right?" I smiled politely and walked away. (Why did I smile?) And when a friend in graduate school, a smart, white, Derridean deconstructionist, upon hearing the happy results of my job search, said, "All the jobs are going to people of color," I was silent.

George Eliot wrote about these pockets of darkness in daily life, the roar on the other side of silence, that most people do not heed and into which we might fall and perish should we pay too much attention. For me, these pockets of darkness do not pass by unnoticed; instead, they implode within, and then self-bind, stitching over their ugliness. For persons of color in America, the imperative to move on in the face of painful encounters comes from a place much deeper than a regard for social niceties. It arises as a claustrophobic survival instinct. It is about carrying on despite the silent tear in the social fabric, the gasping void you must sidestep, or be confronted by the utter rejection of your being and person by the same people smiling around you.

It wasn't until I was on the point of losing everything, all my professional and physical resources and personal havens depleted, that I saw that the tools I have used my entire life to thrive—nose to the grindstone, dedication, discipline, people pleasing, denying my own difference—had been eroding my insides. You dodge one stereotype only to fall into another.

Once, in a university-wide all-faculty meeting, where faculty from all departments across the campus gathered, the topic up for discussion and vote was whether the university should adopt a "Difference and Diversity" requirement for all undergradu-ates. The most vocal resistors opposed the proposition on the grounds that difference and diversity are not academic categories. A political scientist stood up and pronounced, "Scholarship should not be political." Only the white people in the room seemed to be talking. Every scholar of color in that oak-paneled room knew that the moment they spoke, their skin color would immediately disqualify their opinions as self-interest. When a few white colleagues finally stood up to offer counterarguments in support of the proposition, we felt relieved and grateful.

It's a no-win game: as a person of color, you must speak up for yourself, but the moment you speak *as a person of color,* you've already lost the game.

I had been so intent on building a good life, on finding a place for myself, that I hadn't even been aware of the schisms I was unable to bridge. Decorum, duty, and diligence—the perpetual need to prove myself useful—had ordered my days and calibrated my worth, but I had been living, at least partially, someone else's idea of a good life. As a young woman and a woman of color trying to prove herself, I might have been (or thought I was) smart enough to critique and resist institutional power, but in truth I was also invested in success and in being liked. Like they did in all well-bred Chinese girls, my shame and my superego loomed large. They still do. I'm quick to judge myself and others. Most of the time, there are at least two conversations going on in my head and at least one policeman. Most of what's negative in my head gets censored and goes unsaid. I am the kind of person who would never call out a rude salesperson. I simply never return to that store again. With the people in my life, I'm focused and giving but also secretly easily disappointed. If someone fails to reciprocate my goodwill or takes that goodwill for gullibility, I continue to be affable, but my warmth for them dissipates, and they get downgraded in my heart. If all this sounds passive-aggressive, it is because I am.

I was doing this in my marriage, too. I cared too much about my husband not to fight about big issues; there's no downgrading him. But for too many years the painful blowups had trained me (and him, too) to hold off for as long as we could, to allow the difficult thing to go unsaid until it erupted. We kept peace until we couldn't anymore. We kept peace while we slowly became strangers treading on unacknowledged cracks. Hurts and misunderstandings—big, small, real, imagined—gathered and pooled in dark corners. After a while, the threads got too tangled to undo, all the details at once ridiculously petty and heart-stoppingly weighty.

We used to be the couple who transcended and remained untouched and even amused by expectations that would otherwise fray us, from the store clerks who never suspected we were together to the friends who looked faintly surprised when they met our mate, or, closer to home, my father-in-law asking with genuine concern the night before our wedding whether his son really knew what he was taking on. We can do us against the world. But what happens when the world gets between us?

Chinese reticence has not done me much good, but it remains hard to feel like I've the right to talk about myself. When it comes to relationships, that self-effacement is deadly. Every couple has things that remain unsaid between them, but my silences, my cowardice disguised as forbearance, gnaw at my bones, stoking a resentment that my husband doesn't grasp or deserve.

He thought I was more American than I was. I did too.

A student of mine—a young, third-generation Japanese American woman from California, a prelaw A student who was also a gifted opera singer in training, someone seemingly wholly at ease in the world—told me, "Until our class, I didn't know I owned a part of American history." It stunned me. Did *I* feel like I owned a part of American history? After having lived in the United States for almost fifty years and having served as the director of American studies at a major research university for several years, I cannot honestly say that I do. I liked to think that the frisson of being both an insider and an outsider has lent my scholarship its own edge, but really, I never stopped feeling like a stranger, even though I had long ceased to think or dream in Chinese.

My husband hates injustice and unfairness. Yet, at the same time, it seems to me he really doesn't get what it means to be truly powerless, to be faced with social circumstances that defy your best efforts and intentions. How could he? For someone like him—adept, intelligent, determined, white—self-reliance has never let him down, its outcome a just reward. For me, even as I have reaped the benefits of being a "high achiever," I've paid an unspoken price. The immigrant does not own self-determinism the way white privilege does, even if she imagines she shares it, has copied it for her own.

The American immigrant narrative is often told as a tale of exemplary success (stories of reclamation or redemption) or of abject failure (stories of unmitigated vulnerability or precarity). Few talk about the immigrant experience as a series of minor but persistent acts of ordinary and invisible survival, a string of attempts at temporary stability in an imagined, pearly, perfectly borrowed life.

There are a thousand ordinary disasters that roar on the other side of silence and that gently mark our days: the endless distances that stretch intimacy, the invisible accommodations that we make for harmony's sake, the bad moments that give us heartache but that we simply push to get over for fear of an irreparable rip in our social or familial fabric . . . all the barely discernible but disquieting interactions that both enable and inwardly jar the humming rhythm of daily life. Sidestepping those chasms has been a lifework that I am no longer willing to do.

3

Fictions and Frictions
of Interracial Love

1. ROMANCE

Meeting my husband was an event: a singular happening with reverberating waves. He arrived like a stranger whom I should never have known but who somehow clicked into a space that I didn't know was there. Not only was it a miracle that we met at all, since we moved in such different circles, but I was also at a very low point in my life at the time. I was waiting for a divorce to finalize and in the last mental or emotional place on earth to want to meet someone, much less have a relationship.

Marrying the handsomest man I have ever set eyes on six months after meeting him, on the heels of a demoralizing marriage that shook all my confidence in myself as a good judge of character, must sound like a very, very bad idea.

Yet, curiously, I had never been more sure or more at peace. There was a clarity to everything. That's saying a lot, because I doubt and question everything. My ability to see beyond binaries, an asset in my critical work, in real life made me an indecisive and conflicted person. Yet somehow, despite my guardedness, in spite of his unlikeliness (he was too athletic, too techy), I knew early on and very deep in my being that I could put my whole life in his hands.

Falling in love the way the books describe it for the first time in my mid-thirties should have been a recipe for disaster. But after a lifetime of having my feet firmly planted on the ground and having been terribly misled, in my first marriage, by having done the "right" and "clearheaded" thing, being pulled outside of myself in such a surprising way, being thrust on wholly unfamiliar grounds, turned out to be my particular form of salvation, an unsought gift, like rain that you needed but did not ask for.

I knew I was in deep when this man revealed himself to be serious-minded, intelligent, and intense. No one who danced so well or spent so much time honing his athletic skills should be so good at his job, so crazy smart, and so reliable. Like Corian, he was solid, nonporous, the same all the way through. No airs, no vanity, no games, no dissimulation, no finessing. If he doesn't like someone, that person knows, a fact that would later at times vex me but back then felt like an inestimable virtue. My very critical mother likes to say of my meeting my husband: "You fell flat on your face and found gold."

He was the most grown-up man I had ever met. When we first decided to move in together and combine our households, he held a garage sale while I was away on a work trip and sold almost everything he owned. This way you can keep your stuff, he said easily, when I walked, startled, into his empty apartment. The minute we became a team, he did what *we* needed—no guilt trips, no passive-aggression. The world was easy and expansive in his company. A palpable, slightly drunken aura accompanied us wherever we went, buffering our contact with the world. Our connection, unforeseen and organic, wrapped a magical cloak around the two of us. We stood tall and shining. Nothing could touch us.

2. MARRIAGE

Being married means you have seen each other at your most unglorious. My husband has crouched next to me in the cramped bathroom of our first house, holding my hand, while I suffered the worst constipation in the late months of pregnancy. He has cried into my palm the time we lost our unborn baby. He has walked—or rather, half carried—me up and down the driveway when my feet were numb from chemo-induced neuropathy. He has patiently answered the same questions every ten minutes for eight hours while I was stuck in an amnesiac loop, giving me (and him) a scary preview into what Alzheimer's must look like.

Yet, in spite of all this, in spite of his being my miracle person whom I love and trust most in the world, sometimes we go flat and become the White Man and his Asian Wife. It happens in public, like at some dinner party and my husband is being his easy, talkative self, regaling everyone with a description of some invention he concocted in our garage, while I, lazy in my quiet and boring self, bask in the haven his sociability affords me, when I am suddenly jolted into alertness, by some real or imagined glance, that we must look like the typical loud white man and his silent Asian wife. And I prod myself into saying something, anything, just not to be that.

What feels even more devastating is when this happens between us when we are alone. One day he noticed the term *racial capital* in the title of the book I was reading. Not an academic, he hadn't encountered the phrase before. He asked whether the author meant someone who plays the race card (that is, someone who uses their racial identity as a form of currency). I cringed. What a white thing to say. Centuries of white people and institutions had profited from, *made capital out of,* nonwhite persons and bodies, and yet he assumes the "capital" here belongs to the person of color?

To be fair, the phrase is academic jargon and not self-explanatory. He was simply trying to connect an unfamiliar expression to more familiar ones, and he grew up around people for whom "the race card" was just another phrase. But, to me, it was a trigger. How does race, such a fraught and ugly actor, acquire the peculiar status of a game, where what constitutes a winning hand is actually the handicap? Reappearing with the mean caprice of a joker, the race card brings with it a host of revealing questions about the perverse value and perception of race and race matters in America. How else could the terrible, deep wounds of race in this country come to be euphemized as a playing card, a metaphor that acknowledges the rhetoric as such yet simultaneously materializes race into a finite object that can be dealt out, withheld, or trumped? The fact is that someone only is able to play the race card when they have already been excluded from playing in any of the real games that matter. Holding a full deck means being rich with disadvantages.

But how do I say all of this in the moment, short of becoming the Lecturing Professor, a female and hence doubly unpleasant version of what my friend calls a MII (pronounced *me,* and meaning "Men Who Impart Information")? At the moment I was mute, impatient, angry, trying (and failing) desperately not to overreact and have the exchange devolve into a nonproductive fight, where I feel injured and he feels unfairly attacked just by inquiring into a book he sees me reading.

Sometimes I look at my husband and wonder whether he knows to whom he is married.

Yet how could it be otherwise? He grew up a white man in a middle-class family in the middle of white America. His family valued individuality, self-reliance, and their rights to this land. I came from halfway across the world, learned English as a second language, and had parents who thought that teaching through fear and knowing our unbelonging was a good way to keep their children safe. Different forms of love: his parents pushed him out of the nest, for his own good and expansion, while mine wanted to keep my brother and me small, tied to the shadow-width of their wingspan, even at the price of our maturity, because they had moved us all to an unpredictable place without a safety net.

I sometimes dread having conversations with my husband about race. What starts out innocently enough—a chat about a coworker, a discussion about hiring practices, a movie plot—can suddenly turn sour and go south. During the 2016 election, I read about long-married couples filing for divorce because one spouse was a Democrat and the other a Republican. I found such news both shocking and believable. My husband and I are on the same side of the political aisle, and, still, the acrimony of American racial reckoning stings us.

For all our closeness there's an irreducible kernel of difference, of otherness, between us. It erupts like bad weather. The tangible and intangible patterns of training and assumptions sneak in, shape an utterance or a gesture, and take on a life of their own. Over the accretion of dailiness and years, these little beasts pluck at the fabric of our marriage with indifferent appetite.

When I was young I thought that with concerted effort and hard work I could transcend labels that didn't define me. I didn't think of myself as a "woman of color." *That* belonged to victims, not me. Now I wish my husband could see that a foreigner still lives inside of me, that my not-at-homeness is part of who I am and not a matter of choice.

Sometimes I can't believe how politics, a mirage wielded by largely invidious, power-grabbing individuals, could contaminate my most real, weighted, and cherished relationship with someone with whom I've built the only life that matters to me. I suspect that my husband is often hurt that I "allow" external things—world events, intellectual ideas, *things that don't have anything to do with us*—to impact my mood and inflect our private interactions. Yet I also know that, in our world, I live as an unavoidably racialized person. Questions of racial difference, of how people of Asian descent are being seen and treated in this country, past and present, follow me and most likely the future of our children.

In a conversation after Russia's unprovoked invasion of Ukraine, I fretted about Taiwan, which is mainland China's Ukraine. My husband, to comfort me, said the wrong thing: "Stop tying yourself up in knots. Do you even care that much about what happens to Taiwan? You don't have any family there anymore."

I don't know how the man who buttons my winter coat on days that my finger joints are inflamed or who, to this day, always reaches out to take what I am carrying, could also be the man who thinks I wouldn't care about the country from which I came. I was dumbfounded, appalled by his crisp, unmelancholic ability to let things, like the past, go. (Should he ever stop loving me, would he let go of me with equal ruthlessness?) I also realized that there is a huge part of my life about which he knew next to nothing and had little curiosity. He doesn't care much about my past. (Isn't that part of his charm, part of what I fell for?) From his point of view, I've lived three-quarters of my life as an American citizen. I'm a professor of American literature and culture, for goodness' sake. I haven't gone back to Taiwan since he and I met. Why would he think I have attachments there?

Yet those ten-plus years of my life as a child there, chunks of which are blurry even to me, nonetheless form the invisible textures of my being, constituting the secret store of me-ness. In talking about the costs of upward mobility—and, I would add, assimilation—the writer Jennifer Morton uses the term *ethical goods* to name the ineffable, at-risk values of affective bonds with family, community, and a sense of the past that make up our perceptions of who we are. Taiwan is that invisible stock for me: a remembrance of rootedness, of never questioning where I was, of a single me supported by a firm net of grandparents, aunts, great-aunts, and cousins.

My husband is such a presentist, living only in the moment. He doesn't impede himself by looking back and is always moving forward. It's part of his strength, his recovery system. But increasingly I experience myself as a haunted person, being pulled backward, toward what I can no longer see.

The ceaseless sounds of the city below our balcony, the tinny feel of the handle on the pail my brother and I used to carry dumpling soup from the street vendor, my grandparents' stone house in Tainan, the little red balls bouncing on top of water jets in front of the new amusement park outside of Taipei, the queer feelings I got walking among the strange rock formations at Yehliu Geopark, my mother's hand around mine as we strolled down the street, the sight of my father waiting for me at the school gate: when I die, that world, the Taiwan that is only mine to remember, will disappear, too.

3. PARENTING

Twenty years into our marriage and on the cusp of becoming empty nesters, it hit me that almost all of my husband's and my harshest, most explicit fights have circled around issues relating to our children.

How is it I never noticed this before? This realization is shocking and counterintuitive because we have in fact raised two extraordinarily wonderful people. Our children are kind, empathetic, smart, creative, affectionate, even as teenagers. If there is one thing we as a couple are good at doing together, it is parenting. Yet this joint project that has preoccupied us for most of our marriage has taken a tremendous toll on our closeness.

An early, traumatic moment: when he insisted on Ferberizing our two-month-old colicky baby and my hair grew white from her inconsolable, frenetic cries, I think I hated my husband then.

The fissure spread behind the growing years: a conversation about whether taking a break from a bike-riding lesson is appropriate or "coddling" turns into a vortex; a debate about whether we could allow a child to walk the 2.6 miles between the middle school and our home becomes a contest of will and, for me, an anxiety pit; a decision about summer school versus summer jobs a referendum on our core values. What's at stake in these skirmishes? Nothing less than our children's moral character and their future ability to survive in the world.

NOTHING in the world feels as bad as when you think you have to protect your child from your spouse, a soul-grinding choice between betraying your partner and your responsibility toward your children.

My husband is almost always on the side of not pampering the kids, eager for them to grow up, to be self-sufficient and resourceful. I'm almost always on the side of safety, cherishing and safeguarding their already-too-short childhood. He thinks risks breed courage; I think security enables confidence. Maybe this is simply a gender gap, typical father-is-from-Mars and mother-is-from-Venus stuff. But I can't help but think there's a cultural schism here, too, which is to say, a racial difference. His family feels very WASPy to me, with their afternoon cocktails and DIY attitude, while my family feels very Asian, with our ever-present family obligations and extended social duties.

His childhood was filled with house painting, oil changes, deck building, summer jobs; my childhood closed around my sole responsibility, schoolwork. He grew up with the knowledge drilled into him that, after college, he was on his own; sink or swim. I grew up with parents who, even after I was a full-grown, gainfully employed adult, would leave money on my dresser "for parking" after their visits. Trying to pay for a meal for my parents is like battling two indignant generals, while his parents sit back and let him, the independent adult, pay.

Having my parenting instincts questioned by my husband feels horrible because it hurts my deepest feelings and because it feels like I, along with my parents, have been hauled before a judge and found wanting. When my husband wanted to train our babies to "self-soothe" (which I think is just delusional, because if babies could self-soothe, there wouldn't be a thousand lullabies for pacifying babies in every language, nor could Dutailier sell a glider for thousands of dollars), or when he feared that our kids might become "spoiled" or "quitters," I heard an implicit criticism of how I was raised.

I heard, too, my father-in-law, not the charming man he is to me but the brutal parent he was to my husband. He was the kind of father who, on a dead-cold January day in Maryland, sent his young teenage son out in a small skiff in the middle of a lake to see whether he could handle himself. Over the years my husband and his siblings have developed excellent ducking mechanisms. As children they fought not to sit where their father's arm could reach, be it in the car or at the dining table. My husband would tell you himself that the coldest and most miserable times of his life were all spent in the company of his father. Yet I also hear in his voice a note of pride, for having survived and having had a father who instilled in him hard-earned but valuable lessons about strength and fortitude.

Is what I call my husband's "presentism" a reflection of the American can-do, never-look-back spirit or a willful erasure forged out of the burning ore of his father's notions of manhood? Can I separate the two?

What does it mean, anyway, for me to say that race interferes in our marriage? To recognize this is to say everything, and nothing. I'm a scholar of race, but it's still challenging to parse how race lives in the pockets of everyday intimacies. I called his family WASPy, but that's an inaccurate shorthand for the peculiar blend of public and private histories, their manifestations and disguises. My husband grew up hardly ever seeing Blacks, Asians, or foreigners . . . unless, of course, you're talking about his own mother, a Latvian refugee who came to the U.S. at age eleven, right around the same age I was when we emigrated. Unlike the relatively cushioned way I came to the States, my mother-in-law's family had wandered rootlessly across Europe for several years in the wake of World War II, fleeing German and then Russian armies, before making their way to the United States under a refugee sponsorship program. Her family, including her as a child, did fieldwork for three years on a Virginia farm to repay their passage. At age eighty-two now, my mother-in-law is independent, fiercely loyal, and capable of making everything by hand, from curtains to car seat upholstery. She thinks of America as a land of salvation and is susceptible to conservative fearmongering about "immigrant hordes" at the border. She doesn't see the dissonance.

My family, too, practiced its own versions of forgetfulness. My father came to America and didn't look back. He never talked about his childhood and did not own a single photo of himself as a child. I learned from my mother that his father died almost the same time as his birth and that his mother, a young, indigent widow, swayed by some fortune teller, believed that her infant son was the jinx, the cause of her husband's death, when the latter really died from something that penicillin would've prevented. I think that was why my dad became a doctor against his mother's wishes (she didn't want to have to find means of paying for it). My dad pretty much raised himself, put himself through med school, subsisting on a diet of rice balls with dried vegetables that he prepared for himself. Once in America, my father dutifully sent money home to his mother every month for more than two decades in envelopes into which his wife would insert letters on his behalf. He never set foot in Taiwan again.

After my last grandparent died, I never went back to Taiwan, either. I mastered the English language while my Mandarin and Taiwanese Hokkien deteriorated to an embarrassing degree. Neither of my children speak Chinese, and neither have visited Taiwan. (My fault.) My success as an assimilated person depended a great deal on forms of forgetting that I've only now started to come to see. I said I was haunted by history, which is not the same as living consciously with it. History has been a kind of silent creek running in the background of my daily life; only recently has that past risen to meet me like a tidal wave.

Just when I think I've done the hard work of acknowledging that my husband and I as a couple, for all our shiny specialness and individuality, are not immune to the vagaries of politics or ideology, just when I've come to accept that large, impersonal social forces like race can influence and color our most intimate and mundane interactions, the view fractures yet again like a kaleidoscope. The details, once blown up and held close to the eye, become pixelated, at once larger and harder to discern, for "race" encompasses so much: histories (ours and not our own) that touch us; gender disparities; that vague and potent thing called culture; immigration and nationhood; family romance and family idiosyncrasies; familiar plots and unpredictable outcomes.

Psychoanalysis tells us that we all end up marrying our parents, or at least that we're doomed to turn our loved ones into avatars of our parental units. My husband is as different from my dad as you can imagine. One is a relatively traditional Taiwanese man who reserved his hands only for surgery, while the other is a young American DIY guy who loves nothing better than getting oil and dirt under his nails. One is reticent, the other brash; one broods, the other explodes . . . there are a billion ways in which they have nothing in common. Yet both my dad and my husband are survivors of paternal losses, one from absence and the guilt of that absence, the other from an oppressive presence. Both sons grew up and went on to become good family men who put their families first and bore their private pains and discomforts silently and impassively: Chinese and American masculinities with different faces miming each other.

I've resented and leaned on the soldier in my husband. In a crisis, when he goes into his stoic, efficient, combat mode, he bolsters the broken me, but he has no time for my tears or my pessimism. He gets mad at me when I have the common cold as if it were a moral failing on my part, but the moment the C-word dropped into our life, he never faltered by my side. His white family is not untouched by immigrant history, just as he himself is, of course, not untouched by the past.

My husband tells me he has long since forgiven his father. I'm glad but don't trust that he has fully come to terms with the aftershocks. The child in him whom he gladly left behind peeks out from time to time. When his retired father picked up remote-controlled airplanes as a hobby and was trying to master the skill, my husband quickly learned as well; he also researched and built his own planes in order to help his father understand the mechanics. When his father put up a bluebird house, my husband did the same in our yard. He then researched and designed snake guards that he built and sent to his father.

When I see his desire to please his father, I ache for the boy who disappeared. When I hear him telling our son not to cry, especially in front of others, every cell in my body seizes up with anxious protest. *No, no, we're not going to teach our son to hide or repress his feelings; we're not going to teach him shame and toxic masculinity!*

When I overhear my husband talking to our daughter about the damage currently being done to *Roe v. Wade* and its profound implications for our society and her future, I wonder why I ever doubted his parenting instinct. But when I see him pressing our son to go on the roller coaster at the county fair because our son used to be afraid, or whenever my husband tries to muscle his will onto our son, I'm filled with impotent rage and wonder how such a smart person could be so blind.

Our views about childhood itself, as an experience, as a thing, are so vastly different. When people praise our well-behaved children, my husband likes to say, probably after his father, that we discipline our kids to make our own lives easier. I usually let the statement lie without touching it because it frankly sounds like he's speaking a foreign language to me. Is that why we teach our children values, because it is *easier* for us? Since when is our convenience even a consideration when it comes to kids? My father, the ob-gyn, believed that children's needs must take precedence over all adult priorities: in his company, every adult activity must come to a halt should any child in the vicinity need a nap or to eat.

Yet my sentimentality about my golden childhood—about myself as a child—breeds its own selective memories, too. I had two fathers. The one who pulled me behind a closed door to wink at me while my mom expected him to punish me, and who allowed me to scamper up and down his office chair as he talked to patients even as my mom gestured frantically by the door for me to get out. This was the same father who, patient against my mom's resistance, would pack us all up (beach chairs, umbrellas, towels, balls, buckets, lunches, and snacks) to go on the train to explore a new beach along the Taiwan coastline every summer and laugh and scream with us in the waters.

Then there was the father of my teenage years in America: quiet, somber, not prone to silliness, impatient, short-tempered. Although I now know there were many factors at play, it seemed to me then that the older I got, the less light my father became.

My father wasn't someone who yelled or raged, but the dark cloud would descend on him, sucking all the air out of the house. That was when my job would begin: I would top the tightness in my chest with cheerfulness, cajole him with jokes and silly antics, perform cuteness even when I was already too

Author with father and brother at beach

old, because sometimes that worked, sometimes I could tease him out of that darkness.

That was my version of ducking.

Nothing makes my husband the adult more uncomfortable than when I'm being cutesy and childlike, which, unfortunately, is how I take cover. You see the problem.

We come to our children hoping to correct the mistakes of our parents and our own shortcomings, but marriage and parenthood throw us against the rocks of our worst flaws. Our children, I'd like to think, benefited from our differences and our compromises, and certainly neither of us would have sacrificed our chance at parenthood even if we had been told in advance that part of our precious relationship with each other would be the price. I only wish this shared project, this joint and dear investment that we wouldn't have taken on if it weren't for the other, hadn't cost us so much.

4. Recovery

For the first eight years or so of our marriage, we always not only managed to come back together after some fight but were also able to genuinely regroup, as if we had pushed a refresh button. And there we would be again, that shining couple who had found each other against all odds. Now the recovery comes slower, our self-congratulation less radiant, but we are learning that our already-filled hearts still need to grow a few sizes larger.

What you dislike and drives you nuts about your spouse is also what you love and admire. My husband's sexy determinism is also his exasperating stubbornness. His granite strength saves me and throws me into despair. He is Mr. Know-It-All, yet he is full of curiosity. He can act like an asshole but is really generous hearted. (I'm never an asshole, by the way, but I can be mean. When hurt, I lash out viciously, a feral cat cornered in a rusted cage.) He's a bad student because he distrusts authority, yet he thrives on learning new things. He doesn't hold high opinions of academics but is himself a voracious reader. He thinks every doctor and lawyer is out to swindle him, but he would sit in a terrible spot in a restaurant, wait patiently for a waiter determined not to meet our gaze, and overtip because he saw that the waitstaff was thin. He wouldn't call to complain to a service person who was clearly about to stand us up after an eight-hour "window," but he would leave a doctor's waiting room in an indignant huff after thirty minutes. He recently discovered from an X-ray that he must have broken a rib years earlier—at the time he had simply borne the pain without telling anyone—but he is highly sensitive to any "tone" in my voice. He appears more macho than anyone in my world, but he has been a truer partner to me than any of the self-proclaimed feminists I had dated before him. He moved across the country for my job without a second thought. He is an unfairly excellent cook, though if I left the cooking to him, we'd be eating dinner anytime between nine and eleven p.m. He refuses to ask for help even when faced with the most physically daunting tasks, like carrying a refrigerator into the house, but he will patiently research online for different ways to braid our toddler girl's wispy hair with his thick climber's fingers.

How is it possible that this maddening soul is still somehow the one person I most want to see at the end of the day?

You can hurt your long-term partner deeper than you ever imagined is possible. You are prey to the tiniest tremor on each other's moods. You get insanely angry at your partner for not throwing you a lifeline without realizing the other is also drowning. The stakes of all petty things are crazy high because these small, ordinary things are the very fiber of a life you have labored to build together, strand by strand. The enveloping aura that cushioned you has thinned out, become concentrated, now more like an invisible thread that runs between the two of you.

Whether out of a sense of belonging or unbelonging, my husband and I have both bought into the myth of American progress. Doing so has enabled us to accomplish much, but it has also made us ungenerous when one of us stumbles. The intense, seemingly one-off things we argue about unlock larger systems of meaning: forces of family, of race and culture, a wide field of interconnected structures that we can barely perceive most of the time but are always sounding. If we're lucky, we love and fight each other, a small huddle that absorbs and softens the rumbling fields all around us.

Marriage is an exercise in the faith of narrative progress. Its benchmarks—buy a house, have children, see those children through their own life stages, work hard to excel, work hard to retire—train your gaze forward, orienting you toward the next goal as if there were a trophy to be had at the finish line. Popular imagination likes to represent marriage as a long game with a deferred reward program, from the mere paper earned by the first anniversary to the aspirational gold of the mostly impossible fiftieth. But there is no trophy at the end. I read somewhere that there is no happy ending to a marriage: you either split up or one of you dies. I don't, however, take this insight in a maudlin way. There is no forever. We delve into each moment full on, in joy or in angst, because that is *our* moment. Forever is now.

Last week we took our teenage son to an ice cream shop after dinner to celebrate the beginning of summer. The adults were not planning on having anything. My husband has been on a carb-free diet for almost a year. Yes, my crazily strong-willed husband has not had a trace of sugar or a sliver of pasta in months. Me, I was just trying to be good for the night. My son, knowing my weakness, asked me whether I was sure I didn't want anything. I told him that I would have a scoop if they had Tax Crunch, coffee ice cream with almonds and a rich chocolate ribbon that runs through it. It's my favorite from this shop, and they only offer it once a year for a brief period in the middle of April. This was June, so I knew I would be spared from this indulgence. As we waited in line for the lone, harried server, out of the corner of my eye, I saw my husband cross the store to peer into the mini-fridge where they sold prepackaged pints. Anyone would think he was checking out the offering out of vicarious desire, letting his eyes feast on what he has denied himself, but I knew that he was looking to see if there might possibly be a tub of Tax Crunch left in there.

I think of all the hundreds of silent, invisible things he does for me and vice versa. When he comes back to the line, I put my hand in his, like I always do. And, just like that, the thread glimmers.

Part II

Mothers and Daughters

Author's grandmother
as a young woman

Letter to Lin Tsu-Ai,
My Grandmother

Your name meant love, but you did not love me. Everyone knew and seemed to understand that you preferred boys. Boys meant worth and futurity; girls were useless (you raise girls for other people). You found me too skinny, too mouthy, too smart for my own good. Naturally, I became your husband's, my Agon's, favorite: because we were both born in the year of the Tiger; because he thought I took after his brains; and I suspect, if he were honest, because he wanted to tweak you a little.

You tried your best: the awkward hand on my cheek in one photo; the many dresses to tame me; the way you always explained why my brother needed the bigger slice of cake or the extra bun. But I could see the softening of your gaze when you looked at him, the way he could make you smile in ways that no one could coax you to do in a photograph.

It's odd then that years after we moved to America, my most vivid memories of my childhood revolved not around our life in Taipei but around the summers that we spent in your house in Tainan. Maybe summers are always more memorable for kids. Maybe it is because your house was so extraordinary, the stuff of exploration: a white stone building standing three stories high, with balconies, a rooftop terrace, three interior courtyard gardens (one with a real well), complete with a mysterious and slightly scary vacant back compound where servants used to live, and the long-unused water gully set along the perimeter that bred mosquitoes and made the best guide to run along.

Every summer you would summon your daughter home. My mother would pack up my brother and me, leave my father behind, and take the train southward. That ride (now two hours on an express train) used to take six to seven hours, but my brother and I loved it. We knew all the landmarks by heart: the wet, tiered rice paddy fields that would appear the moment the city receded, the Eagle Rock that anticipated Taichung, the mid-way point. Trains in those days boasted dining cars with crisp white tablecloths, a vase on each table, and such great food that reputedly people would take the train just to eat. Even the bento boxes that came by on steel carriers were delicious, especially the grilled pork chops with pickled vegetables. To my mother's frustration every time, my brother and I would bounce off our seats only to start to wilt just before the train pulled into Tainan, and then she would have to contend with luggage and two half-asleep kids.

By the time we got to your house, we would be totally awake again. While you fussed over Mom and my brother, I would rush upstairs to Mom's old room. First, I checked on my friends in the glass bookshelf: the little wooden Dutch milkmaid whose butterstick is really an hourglass; the neat queue of Kokeshi dolls; the kissing Dresden salt and pepper bride and groom; the miniature purple Mandarin duck whose back sported tiny holes for a jasmine flower or two. The bookshelf smelled of strange and faraway places. Then I would, at last, turn to the head that hung to the side of the shelf—not really a head but the ceramic face of a foreign little girl with big, flat blue eyes, cherry-red lips, and a headful of yellow curls. Years later, in America, I would learn that it was Shirley Temple, whose likeness was sold to adoring mothers and daughters all over the world. Back then, I found her shiny, anonymous face with its stark colors slightly repulsive but fascinating. I would carefully take it down, turn it over, and trace with my fingers the white, hollow backside that looked like a concave face; the contact made me inexplicably queasy. My mom told me that when she was a little girl, she wanted nothing more than to look like that girl. Once she sat patiently for hours while you, Amah, curled her hair with a heated rod. The result, according to her, was disappointing.

Those summer days we spent in Tainan with you felt long and luxurious, cloistered in time, imprinted with sun and moisture. The hours were mostly marked by our stomachs: the small eels that one can buy only in Tainan, poached with ginger to delicate perfection for a special afternoon treat; the sweet tofu bought from the vendor whom you paid extra for an additional spoonful of brown sugar to the soup; the six-course meal every night; your homemade vanilla ice cream served between the square monaka shells that melted in the mouth. You did not like me in the kitchen, but you did teach me to sew. I think I got some of my unforgiving perfectionism from those lessons. Once I rushed through a dress I was eager to wear, proud of my own speed. You came along, turned the dress inside out, inspected the workmanship, and calmly ripped the seams apart. The stitches were uneven and the inseams inconsistent; do it over, you said. Your eye and hand for precision and detail were the stuff that family legends were made of: those tiny, barely inch-tall, faceless, silk clown dolls that you made in a rainbow of colors and placed in miniature glass jars (see Figure 1 of insert); the dark red velvet

Author's mother as "Shirley Temple"

baby shoes with the kitten lining inside and hand-stitched backing, the rows of stitches looking machine-made (Figure 2).

Although it was never overt, you and I butted heads all the time. Like how, in those summers, in spite of my begging, you would not allow my mother to wake me up from my afternoon naps; I would always wake up sweaty and alone behind the mosquito netting, while I could hear the rest of the family downstairs, talking and laughing, already having had midafternoon snacks together. Or how you kept asking Agon not to let me follow him around the house while he fixed things, because girls don't mess with tools. Or, later, after we moved to the United States, how during your visits you would complain to my mom about my darkening skin in the Georgia sun. "Why do you allow her to go to the beach all day? She looks like a peasant!" I remember being embarrassed by your old-fashioned biases, but I also remember feeling shame.

As a teenage immigrant, I could barely find my place among American ideas of femininity, and I had already bungled Chinese girlhood. In Tainan, you, your sisters, and my mother were all known, both inside and outside of the family, as great beauties. I looked nothing like you. In this, too, I failed you. You always had to explain to people that I took after my father. One time, my mother took me aside to tell me, "You know, you don't have beauty, but you have likability, and that is more important." (The Taiwanese term for *likable* takes three words and means, literally, "begging for care.") Well, maybe, but not what a six-year-old girl wants to hear from her mother.

You and I fought to the end. When I went to see you after your stroke, were you disappointed that it was not my brother who came? When your jaw first relinquished its hold, you stopped eating and talking. You would rather commit to silence and hunger than dribble your words or food. It must have been cruel for someone who used to iron her handkerchiefs and bed linens to find herself drooling, unable even to bathe herself. Wiping down your loose skin and jutting bones, I would feel the air being squeezed out of my lungs. (*This* belonged to someone who believed that being plump is a sign of fortune.) Even then, you remained sharp, asking after the mailman's timely arrival, noting the exact day of the week without the help of a calendar. Your handwriting on the small white pads, distinct and elegant, like hawks thrusting through air, demanding their wild fields. You did not understand why we were fighting to keep you. You wanted so much to be released, and we could not allow it. During the force feedings, your fingers gripped my wrists like small, angry ferrets—anger, for love's severity; anger, for the body that continues to need tending.

At night, in the other room, I counted your ragged breaths. One evening, I found you crying. I sat down to cry with you. You wrote something on your pad. I thought you wanted to comfort me. Instead, you wrote, "I am glad you are crying. I do not want to be alone."

Now I'm the one facing the end of time. Disease (cancer, a global pandemic, racism) stitches and unstitches my days. Although I continue to do all I can to stay alive, I finally understand something of your refusal. When chemo was erasing me with its indifferent and brutal malaise, there were days when, in the silent recesses of my mind, I wished I could just *stop being*. This is something I could never fully admit, even to myself, because it feels deeply ungrateful, because it feels like a betrayal of my job as parent and partner.

In chemo time, everything falls away except the barest love. But in world time, love is hard to be had. I live in an unimaginable moment when the entire world is also facing a health crisis, and the country that I have come to call my own is besieged by fires, floods, and civil unrest from coast to coast. And instead of caring for one another, old hates thrive. I feel my vulnerability every day. And I fear the multiple toxicities (viral, political, cultural, and environmental) that threaten the future of my children.

Years ago, I wrote in my academic work that America suffered from a racial melancholia it could neither swallow nor digest, that unprocessed grief hidden behind grievances continues to haunt our social relations, that the discourse of racial *identity* has obscured the history of American racial *entanglements*. More and more, I think there is no getting over three centuries of American racial strife, and the enduring, knotted legacy of systemic and cultural racism. But I have to ask, in the absence of love, what *is* possible?

Amah, my world is so different from yours in a thousand ways. And in real life, we would never be having this conversation. You did not live in a world where people talked about race or racism, or even about love. You would be mystified by what preoccupies my thoughts. The truth is I do not remember ever having had a conversation with you beyond passing, quotidian exchanges. But, once, the day before I left you to return to the States, you sat up in bed and allowed me to brush your hair, undyed and brittle, still startlingly thick, each strand seemingly alive with its own will. I managed to twist it into a neat bun. I powdered your face, put on some light blush and a thin coat of lipstick.

You looked up at me with those huge dark lynx eyes of yours, made even more preternatural by weight loss, and I thought I saw something like pleasure.

Weeks after the news arrived, here in America, I found myself confessing your passing to almost everyone I saw—the mail carrier, the gas attendant, the fruit stand checker. I knew they were strangers; I knew it was TMI. Something in the recitation made your vanishing, halfway across the world, less ephemeral. People offered sympathy; some shared their own losses. Looking back, I was too young then, even in my early thirties, to grasp all the ways in which suffering and loss can create company, how intimacy can be forged between strangers, and that just because something is fleeting or provisional does not mean it is not doing some work.

Amah, I want to be able to say, in the common grief of strangers, I have not left you alone.

5

Irascible Love

During the worst of the pandemic, I FaceTimed with my mother. (This was before that source of communication became impossible, back when I could still get her to respond to the green button on the screen.) She would tell me how tired she is of this life, how everything around her (the internet, the race talks, the weather) feels so foreign to her. She said, *I am a stranger to this life,* weaving her head side to side in an uncharacteristically inelegant fashion as if she were trying to break free of some invisible threads.

I couldn't accept this morose, needy woman. For most of my life, my mother had remained coolly composed. Photos of her—as a young woman, a wife, a mother of young and then not-so-young children—show a remarkably unchanged woman. There's a cartoon out there on the internet about the Pretty Asian Woman who never ages until suddenly, poof, in the last frame, as if overnight, she grows plump, loses half of her height, and starts to wear nothing but tracksuits. But even in her mid-seventies, my mother remained slender, her hair dyed but thick, and the most elegantly dressed woman in town. Before Covid-19, she went to the gym every day and ballroom dances three times a week. The first time I saw a change in her appearance was when we unexpectedly lost my father to lung cancer more than fifteen years ago. She walked about for a few years looking like a piece of glass that had cracked but not yet fallen. Even so, she regrouped and went on living in a way that I'm not sure my father, reputedly the stronger one, would have been able to had the situation been reversed.

Everyone, including my mother and me, believed in the myth of our closeness, so much so that it was always said that we looked like sisters, even though we both knew that I looked nothing like her. We would laugh about it, just between us, as if our enviable intimacy pulled the wool over everyone's eyes and made us, indeed, look alike.

At what point did she become a stranger to me? Her increasing anxiety and need for reassurance about everyday things—the arrival of a package, the safety of her practically new car, the idea of my driving on a rainy day or flying for work—sat on me like a weighted blanket. I was ashamed but could not prevent the rising tide of edginess in my voice when she called me about expiring airline miles, how to spell the word *thermostat,* the gecko that got in the house and terrorized her all night. It drove me crazy that she refused to leave messages on the phone and would simply keep calling every thirty minutes until I picked up. I was frustrated by her refusal to learn anything new, however minute, like how to change the clock in her car or how to close a web page on her iPad. When I asked her whether she calls my brother, who lives but three miles from her, as often as she calls me, she responded with surprise, "Of course not. He has an important job, you know."

Her ageless exterior had been deceptive. At first, it seemed as if someone had made a photographic likeness of her and smeared the outline, just a little. Her joy and interests in things, even shopping, grew blunted, just as her hearing had. During the early days of the pandemic, I noticed that Taiwanese worked better with her, but talking to her exhausted me not only because I had to shout and repeat myself but also because it felt like, at least in my exasperation, she was jealously demanding my attention without really wanting it.

It's easy to attribute the change (in her or in me?) to my father's illness. Before, she was the implacable surface that absorbed my father's sudden storms, my brother's stubbornness, and my hypersensitivities. It had taken me by surprise when my father was first diagnosed and she reacted with what looked like self-ishness. All through the ordeal of his illness, he was stoic while she complained about inconsequential things. When I couldn't travel across the country to see my dad anymore because I was drawing close to my due date after having had a miscarriage the year before, I had to rely on the phone. My mom would dominate the calls, and it seemed that all she could talk about was her suffering: how on those long trips up to Baltimore for the clinical trials, my father was grumpy and unhelpful, or how the motel didn't have room service so she was forced to cross two highways on foot on those cold, dark nights in order to buy dinner for the two of them, which he refused to eat anyway. I didn't want to hear about any of that. My worries for my father and my own guilt about not being there left little room for anything else.

Later I realized that my and everyone else's focus on my father at the time must have spurred her self-focus. She was drowning, and no one noticed. She was at the heart but not the center of the crisis.

In one history, my mother appeared small and submerged, and I was her unsolicited champion. A family lore of triumph among our relatives, for example, revolved around my father, my brother, and me: how my father left a successful surgical and academic career in Taiwan to start over in the United States as a resident and eventually rebuilt a thriving practice; how my brother and I learned English from scratch as teenagers; how my brother became a doctor, too, and how I went on to become a professor of English literature. Tales of immigrant success. But the real story could've been how my mother learned English at all. Without the benefit of a college education (like my dad) and without the aid of ESL teachers (like us kids), she learned English on her own, on the fly, struggling to communicate with grocers, flipping through her pocket-size English-Chinese dictionary, watching *The Price Is Right* and *All My Children*. I used to joke that it's a miracle she didn't speak in soap-opera hyperboles all the time. But, really, how was it none of us ever thought about how my mother would learn English?

When she turned a marriageable age, her previously indulgent father gave her three choices for a husband and then pushed hard for the (poor) young man whom he thought (mistakenly) he could control. My father, whom I loved dearly, was not an easy person, by turns incisive and caustic, teasing and brooding, generous and critical, affectionate and inflexible. I used to watch his moods the way a meteorologist watches the skies. And although the world would know him as a stern man, we knew in our little circle that he was capable of great bursts of surprising, infectious, childlike mischievousness, making his descents into stormy darkness all the scarier even as they made his light self, when it returned, that much more charismatic.

With my mother, he was both doting and condescending. He

mocked her unworldliness even as he worked hard to keep her that way. His care of her was meticulous and far-seeing, yet at times he thought nothing of deriding her lack of education or sense. Once, after a particularly stormy outbreak because he lost his own keys and blamed her, I, the young feminist home from college, ratcheted up my courage to shout at my father and told her that she did not have to put up with it. She looked at me in frustration and said angrily, "What do you want from me? Divorce him? I *cannot* do that."

Later, while I was still fuming upstairs on her behalf, I saw her out the window below, weeding the flower bed. My father had walked up silently and knelt down beside her to start to weed as well, their hands at first jerky and then growing into a smooth rhythm.

In another history, my mother loomed large and intentional. She ruled our days and nights. She was there for every meal, every cut and bruise, but she was never one for playing games or coddling hurt feelings, her lack of sentimentality the bracing yardstick against which I judged my own emotional messiness.

She liked to tell this joke about how, as a little girl, I would wake up from summer naps in my grandfather's maze of a house in Tainan and wander from room to room, murmuring, "Mama, Mama . . . ," looking for her with increasing distress until I burst into tears, and then she would finally show herself. She would repeat the story and chuckle about how easy it was for her to stay hidden in any given room just by being silent, because in my rush to find her I would barely step into a room before running to the next. I would laugh along with the story while feeling hurt and humiliated.

When I was six, leaning against her legs while she sat in front of her vanity doing her makeup, something I used to love to watch her do, she told me while brushing one perfectly arched eyebrow that, when she first learned she had a daughter, she cried with bitter disappointment in the hospital room while my father was out in the corridor bragging about me. I don't have that many memories of our daily life in Taipei, as if immigration and learning a new language had wiped clean much of what had gone on before, but I remember that moment clearly, looking up at her through our reflections in the tall mirror, hearing the roar in my ears and feeling the distance stretch and freeze between us. I remember blinking hard, willing my face still, wanting both to run away from her and to remain by her side as her confidante.

There would be other such admissions, like how my father was not her choice even though it turned out all right; how she once had a boyfriend, someone she loved and never forgot, the one who died. These little revelations folded me into the precious orbit of her interiority even as they banished me from it.

My mother thinks candor is an overrated, American value. She prefers to have her communication layered over, adjustable, and softened with ambiguity. This means I can never tell, at any given moment, what is real and what is made up. Sometimes her prevarication grows out of politeness, the normal Taiwanese kind where you say you are full even when you're starving. Sometimes it is born out of a deeply honed sense of strategy: how best to present yourself to an always public eye, how you position yourself and others. This makes trying to gauge her real desire and opinion time-consuming and almost always unsuccessful. Every gift I give her risks days of gratitude along with convoluted explanations of why the thing is too special or valuable, too delicate or weighty, for use.

Speaking with my mother is sometimes like dealing with an ambassador from a small country: you are plagued by the suspicion that you have not done enough even though her smile remains gracious.

I wonder how we would communicate were she to forget her English altogether and I my Taiwanese. Taiwanese is such an old and oddly specific dialect. Every character has eight intonations—as opposed to Mandarin, which has four—each generating a different meaning. One word with one accent can mean "bitterness"; the same word with a different accent means "to savor." And each word can hold tender nuances. There is, for instance, a single verb that describes a particular quality of cherishing, referring to an object so precious that it precludes its own use. So you fold the thing up carefully, wrap it in plastic, and put it in the bottom of your drawer. Maybe this is why sometimes I cannot tell the difference between saving something and throwing it away.

My American education and career must have looked like an unspoken critique of my mother's life. I didn't choose her path as a housewife and a mother, at least not for a long time. When I finally had my own daughter, in my late thirties, my mother came for a visit. She watched me play on the kitchen floor with my little girl and said, "I am glad you are enjoying this. I never did." I felt sad for her, and then for me.

I understand, I really do, and I grieve for all the choices (whom to marry, how many children to have, what country to live in) that were not hers for the making. That terrible lesson that girls are not worth the meals you feed them came from her mother and her mother before her, a female legacy. Men don't say it. They don't need to. The women, though, repeat it, fold its truth deep within, become its custodians. This, too, is survival.

But somewhere in me there must have been a wish that my mom could have freed herself from the grooves of her training, that in saving tiny parts of herself she could have saved me, too. I'm always surprised by the rush of this hope. It gets me in trouble again and again. Once, in my twenties, I came home from graduate school for a visit. I went out with my mother, just the two of us, to an elegant lunch by Savannah River. There we were, two grown women, dressed up like southern-women-who-lunch, like friends. It was a warm, expansive day. I took the plunge and told her about my first serious broken love affair. The sun shone behind her, glinting off the water. I could see the reddish tints at the edges of her dark chestnut hair glowing like a halo around her head. She shrugged her shoulders, said with a slight frown, "Why would you want someone who doesn't want you?" Then she changed the subject.

What hurt the most was that she didn't seem at all surprised that someone had rejected me.

It feels like a kind of necessary killing, this business of being mothers and daughters, a compulsory paring down or a sacrifice of our full selves in order to be there for the other. Recently, my mother brought up that young man again, her old love . . . this time spurred on, of all things, by seeing the film *Crazy Rich Asians*. She called me in a state of agitated excitement to tell me that she saw the movie, and in Henry Golding's visage she came face-to-face with her dead boyfriend. "It was like seeing a ghost," she said.

It was all too much for me: the flood of what was lost to her so long ago and to her whole life; the emergence of a past denied halfway across the world erupting in this moment on the big screen; the whitewashing of her memories; the fantasy and the reality; the ways in which my father, and therefore I, never belonged in her story. I had never known how to respond to her in these kinds of moments. I murmured something incomprehensible in response and quickly got off the phone.

I wished she wouldn't confide such things to me. Then one day, it struck me that this was her version of sharing, and I had responded to her much as she had to me by the river.

These days she backpedals a lot, going out of her way to tell me effusively how wonderful daughters are, how daughters are much more sensitive, caring, and "fine-nerved" than sons, while I wonder whether she has really changed her mind or if she is flattering me to keep my care.

When I was going through chemo, she reached out to tell me she had an annuity to which she wanted to add my name as the sole beneficiary. I found it odd that she should be trying to leave me money at a point when I might be dying, but I told her that everything should be divided equally between my brother and me, as my father's will had stipulated. She said no, this was not part of the estate but money that my father had set aside separately and invested on my behalf decades ago after he had given a piece of land to my brother. *Baba said your brother's medical school was much more expensive, and you know how Baba was always worried about your future.* (The latter, I gathered, because I had no "real skills.") For months, she talked endlessly about this, even though I had very little mental room for such a topic. Then she informed me that my brother and his wife had "somehow" found out, and they were not happy. I suggested again that she simply add my brother's name as a co-beneficiary. She came back with an insistent no, absolutely not; don't worry; this was *her* call, and what my dad wanted. A week later, during our Zoom Thanksgiving dinner (because Covid), between bites, she said casually, "Oh, your brother added his name to the annuity." I said, "Good."

This was exactly what should have happened, but inside a heavy curtain fell. A tight, familiar knot grew in my chest. I had the irrational sense that the cells deep inside me were getting sick again. It was only afterward that I realized I had taken her initial gesture to be a token, a silent way of telling me that she wanted to prioritize me. Did I fall for the imagined outstretched hand again? Had my father tried, however misguidedly, to think of me beyond his days? Was this whole episode a gambit for my attention? Was any of it—her desire, her attempts, my brother's role—real?

The morning after that Thanksgiving dinner, when I was still feeling raw, my mother called in distress because she had somehow lost the icon for the Friends Locator app I had installed on her phone. I had had the not-so-brilliant idea that it would give her some comfort, to lessen her anxiety, to be able to check my location at any given time. And by the endless "Mom likes your location" alerts I got, I could tell that she used the app frequently. But then somehow the little square tile had disappeared from her phone. I could hear the panic in her voice. She couldn't tell where I was, even though I was on the other end of the line.

For fifteen insane minutes, I could not get her to tap on the link I sent her to re-download the app. (I added "Do not ask for tech advice unless willing to listen" to my "Things Not to Do to My Daughter When I'm Old" list.) My mother kept talking over me on the phone, struggling to read the URL to me as if it were a sentence that she needed me to translate. I could not get her to listen to me, not even in Taiwanese.

My mother is right when she says she is a stranger in this world. I fear that she's losing not just her hearing but also her English, the way that aging people shed skills, in reverse order of their acquisition. English would be the first to go, then the cursory Japanese she learned as a child during the Japanese occupation, then her Mandarin, leaving her at last with her native Taiwanese, a tongue few around her speak.

I think back on those post-nap afternoons in Tainan so long ago when my mother and I first started this game of hide-and-seek: a young mother eager to carve out a few seconds of separateness, even at the price of having then to console a crying child, and a child shuttling between blind trust and the fear of abandonment. These two will reprise and switch roles across time and geography, across worlds. I desperately want to keep them in the same picture even though they're really each only discernible in separate frames, both following a pitch out of the realm of hearing, groping for home base.

6

The Look

1.

I was fourteen and lost in front of a particularly alluring pair of shoes in a shop window in the mall (Figure 3). I felt my mom's hand at my elbow urging me away. I thought it was her way of saying no to the shoes until I looked up and followed the line of her gaze: an adult white man was staring at me from outside the other corner of the store, his neck strained forward through two panes of glass. He did not see my mother watching him watching me. It was the kind of look that was at once concentrated and abstract; the thrust of it seemed to bore right through me to a point behind me, making me at once obdurate and transparent.

A few years later, I would remember that look, when on the Métro in Paris I found another white man looking at me with the same kind of intense, blank stare that made me wish I was thousands of miles away. Back then, an older Parisian friend had cautioned care, explaining that there were French men who still thought Asian women were prostitutes. I remember being shocked by the bizarre assumption. Since then, I have come to learn the deep histories of French colonial rule in "Indochina" and, in my own adopted country, the prevailing nineteenth-century American notion, at times even written into laws, about pestilential Chinese prostitutes. In the twentieth century, U.S. masculine and militarized presence in Asia spawned its own expansive racial-erotic imagination, stoking for more than two centuries this sexual notion about Asiatic femininity. Now, this association between Asian femininity and crass availability in Western, masculine imagination seems to me far from eccentric.

At fourteen, I was too naive to suspect that such a gaze might have been sexual. I had thought such looks must be filled with scorn or hate. Now, knowing that sexual desire does not preclude racial disdain, I recognize that those looks could have been, and mostly likely were, combinations of both.

I hate how that mix of derision and desire still instills fear in me. Anger would be preferable. I grew up in the United States with most of the freedoms that my immigrant parents wished for me, but my American Dream would be punctuated at the edges by fleeting encounters that no longer surprised me but have never ceased to reach the pit of my stomach. Strange white men who cooed, "Me love you long time"; unsolicited reminiscences of men who were "once stationed in Vietnam or Korea"; the unwanted ni hao ma or konichiwa when I walked down the street; coffee dates with myself interrupted by slips of notes that announced "I adore Asian women"; being told I was beautiful when I knew that was not what was meant.

Years later, as a professor on my first day of teaching at a prestigious East Coast university, I was heading to my first lecture, armed with my syllabus and my game face, when a young blond man, clearly an undergraduate, bumped hard into my shoulder with a breezy "Ni hao ma" tossed in his wake. My brain froze. Was this another one of those creepy men, or simply a student taking a Mandarin class?

2.

I have never been able to reconcile my deep discomfort with being seen by strangers with my love for clothes. How is it that someone who has been trained by the world that it is better not to be noticed can also be someone who enjoys sartorial play? Can I be a feminist and still love fashion? Can a woman of color participate in acts of beauty without self-harm? What is beauty for the "unbeautiful"?

People always assume that women dress for others, as a gambit for attention, either for the admiring male gaze or the envious gaze of other women. And if a woman were to dress "just for herself," it must be a form of narcissism. A woman with sartorial preoccupation must be either a hapless victim (prey to commodity culture and patriarchal expectations) or a cunning performer (someone who refashions herself at will). And when it comes to a woman of color, whose relationship to commodified sexuality is so fraught and historically compromised, it is especially difficult to talk about beauty and style without making her either self-objectifying or plain uppity. We can probably all safely debate the beauty of a thing—a flower or a painting—without too much heat, but when it comes to the beauty of a person, especially a woman of color, we are suddenly in a minefield of objectification, fetishization, and appropriation, at risk from others and from ourselves.

A friend once noted that he thought *the* question that every woman must face is the question of beauty. Even if a woman ultimately decides to reject beauty, he said, it remains the question that every girl-becoming-woman must negotiate. I was not so sure a woman could reject beauty even if she wanted to, because the issue is not her response but the injunction implicit in the question. But I took his point and asked what he thought *the* question would be for men. He thought about it and said, "Probably the question of jobs, career, his moneymaking potential." This all sounds old-fashioned, yet probably not far from what is still true.

In ancient Greece, the word for adornment, *kosmos,* means both "decoration" and "world order." This is why the words *cosmetics* and *cosmology* share an etymological root. Presumably there was a time when the act of self-adornment was not seen as shallow or superficial but as originating from a desire to have the human body echo and be in tune with the invisible forces of the universe: the body as world and the world as body. In this view, the decorated human body itself serves as a carrier, a micrograph, of the visible world. (In modern Greek, a gossip is someone who will tell your business to the whole *kosmos,* reminding us that "makeup"—putting a face on—is connected to a kind of citizenship, a signing up to participate in the glamor of sociality.) The ornament of clothing, far from being inert or fake, promised to expand the body's periphery, extending its connection to the world. We humans, especially women, have long lost that sense of undividedness from the world.

Maybe that kind of connection was always no more than a human wish, but surely there was a time during human development when such at-oneness with the world existed. Psychoanalysts postulate what they call the oceanic or, rather aptly, pre-mirror stage, when you do not yet see your own reflection as an Other. For a woman, that moment could only be pre-womanhood, before a girl has to think about *having a relationship* with her body. There's this story that my mother loves to tell about the time I went to my elementary school in Taipei not only out of uniform but also wearing the most garish outfit. That year my grandparents had returned from their annual trip to America and brought back for me the surprising gift, not of more dresses, but of a pantsuit. The top was bright canary yellow, made from some synthetic, textured fabric that was in truth a little itchy but reminded me of a sea of bubbles. The shirt sported sharp button-down collars and a long, wide, bright orange tie. The sleeves ballooned out extravagantly, like bells, only to cinch back in tightly at the wrist by a row of five small, covered buttons. Then there was the bottom: a pair of front-seamed, bell-bottom pants, in orange, of course.

I had never seen anything so cool in all my life. I insisted on wearing this glowing yellow-orange mirage to school, even though it was school picture day. My mother warned me that she would not come get me at school or make excuses for me should I be sent home. I told her not to worry. To this day, my mother does not know, nor do I recall, what tale I spun to get the teachers to allow it. Somewhere out there in photo grave-yards there is a photograph of two neat rows of Taiwanese kids in black and white uniforms . . . and then me, in my bright yellow and orange bell-bottom suit and tie.

3.

I miss that girl, not because she enjoyed being seen but because she didn't care that she was. Her pleasure in that outfit was more felt than remembered. Imagine that: to be so at home in the world, so undivided from your own body, that what you wear is but an extension of *being in the world.*

Maybe it is in nostalgia, or simply in compensation for that memory of lost plenitude that, as an adult, I am particularly drawn to clothes that are world-making: sartorial constructions that seem to generate milieus of their own, clothes so meticulously constructed that they seem capable of standing alone, sometimes even *standing in* for the human body. I am thinking of those creations that are so saturated with narrative possibilities that the human wearer becomes their embellishment rather than the other way around: Kim Novak's auratic gray suit in *Vertigo,* Maggie Cheung's architectural chipaos, Emma Peel's unpeelable body suits, Iris van Herpen's stark bone dress (Figures 4–7).

These creations, though different in context and time, share one quality for me: an object-expressiveness, a thingliness so ontologically suggestive that it survives in the imagination, acquiring an inner life beyond the women or characters accompanying them.

What seduces the eye and the mind here is not the fleshly female body per se but the allure of the supplemental becoming primary, of the inanimate that has grown sensorial and gorgeous. It's not a coincidence that these sartorial revenants veer toward *costume:* not because they are fantastical or artificial but because they amplify and celebrate that unnerving gap between body and dress, person and persona, human and thing.

Wearing these creations, one can be both more and less oneself.

A woman can hide in that gap, a pocket of becoming.

Fashion has always teetered between the need for uniqueness

and the demand for mass production, between art and market. In the early twentieth century, the German philosopher Walter Benjamin used the term *aura* to refer to the unique originality of a work of art, highlighting art's onetime presence in a specific time and space. Benjamin thought that we, in the twentieth century, had lost the magic of aura because in an age of accelerated mechanical reproduction, art can be reproduced, bought, and exist anywhere, anytime, as a copy. But I wonder if a concept like glamor, a conscious engagement of artifice and itself often a citation of other recognizable figures (like Lady Gaga citing Madonna citing Marilyn Monroe), might hold out for us some possibilities for aura today? Unlike beauty, which is often idealized, naturalized, and thought to be God-given (in spite of its being heavily socially, culturally, and racially determined), glamor is not apologetic about its artifice. Instead of deadening reproducibility or natural authenticity, glamor is all about the enchantment of *synthetic malleability* . . . and its potential for surviving in repetition.

This is why the outfits in Figures 4–7 are both glamorous and potentially "auratic." While all of them can and have invited copies and imitations, each subsequent replica (and each subsequent wearer) can only fulfill these outfits' most intense fantasies by harking back to the idea of some possible, originary presence: a reproduction that allows you to inhabit, just a little, the auratic space of the imagined original. Without such promise, a gray suit is just a gray suit. (In *Vertigo,* Novak's Madeleine will herself turn out to be a spellbinding counterfeit, a copy of a charismatic but lost, or simply nonexistent, original.) These sartorial creations are thus imbued, not so much with beauty as with a specific and slightly decentering flirtation with the dream of *presence:* an act of adornment/covering that renders selfhood visible to the self.

I like to think of this kind of aesthetic pleasure not as something that only invites consumption but also as an experience that triggers a psychical transaction, one in which our sense of being a person transitions, deliciously and precariously, into our sense of being a thing, and vice versa. The British cultural theorist Rachel Bowlby, who writes smartly about the experience and history of shopping, once described the checkout counter as a moment of anxiety, of de-transcendence, when you fall from shopping's pleasures of hunting and gathering into the reality of having to pay. I think of the moment of getting dressed, of the "checkout" moment in the dressing room, as a similar though much more potential-filled moment: a psychical exchange when you have given up a little of yourself in order to be a little of the thing you love, and in being that thing, you become a little more yourself.

Of course, that room for play—that slippery moment between *who* and *what* you are—is tricky. There is both freedom and danger in sliding between being a person and being a thing, especially for a woman of color, who is always already made into an object (of desire, of use, of denigration). It is politically dicey to talk about a woman finding escape in being thinglike. But, sometimes, for those bodies made heavy by mainstream cultural fantasies, disappearing into synthetic self-extensions—that is, fashion—can provide a temporary relief from the burdens of having bodies and their inevitable weighty visibility. Sometimes you cover yourself up in order to reveal more of yourself, and sometimes the covering relieves you of being you.

Those who have been deemed unusual- or odd-looking tend to turn to the resources of glamor, because glamor, as a particular form of extravagant cloaking, has the potential to liberate women—not by providing a shield of desirability (because desirability also makes women vulnerable) but, rather, by extending them a temporary guise that saves them from the burdens of "authentic personhood." I suspect women from Bette Davis to Josephine Baker to Stefani Germanotta know this well.

4.

All of this may explain why I had such a moment of consternation—something between recognition and recoil—one day in the Metropolitan Museum of Art when I was confronted by this sculpture (or is it a garment?) made by contemporary Chinese artist Li Xiaofeng (Figure 8).

This is Beauty, and this is Ugliness. This is femininity elevated to the status of (not-to-be-used) Art and (to-be-used) debased Things. Composed wholly of shattered ceramics, this dress, according to the placard, was made to be actually "wearable." But to wear this is to put on the weight and shape of *another, already existing body:* one dreamed up by history, a body that is the residue of centuries of ideas about Asia, femininity, porcelain-imaginary, domesticity, the burdens and privileges of person-as-art/thing.

Is this Chinese femininity or its arrested development? Armor or exposure? Winged victory or grounded flight? Devastation or recuperation? Antiquing or dumpster diving?

Maybe this woman-thing is bearing a form of witness, testifying to the continuities belied by these dyads. Maybe this *is* Chinese femininity on display for and in the West, a stranded but still-standing shell that bears the fractures of its making.

Maybe this is what survival looks like.

5.

When my daughter turned eighteen, I started to make mental notes of things I want to tell her but can't. I have not told her, for instance, that in the hospital when she was born, holding such love in my arms, I thought that if I were to die in her arms one day, I would be content. I have not told her this because it is terribly morbid and selfish. For similar reasons, I have also not been able to bring myself to tell her about the kind of gaze and encounters that I confessed here. It's not only that I think certain life experiences cannot be passed on; it's also that I am always struggling between preparing my kids for the real world and protecting them from its toxicities.

My daughter's childhood was spent in a small but cosmopolitan town. Her preschool class of twelve had only one monoracial child, and he was a Swedish national. Whereas my middle school history book in Georgia devoted its chapter on the Civil War primarily to the invention of the cotton gin, my daughter at age six was already explaining the word *segregation* to her younger brother. When both marveled together at what seemed to them an unimaginable universe where such inequality could exist, I realized how better educated they are about American racial history than I was, but also how, by being habituated to the virtues of diversity, they remain innocent about the still-brutal realities of racism.

My daughter grew up with love, privilege, and an ease with the world that has allowed her to be an affectionate, demonstrative child who has also been able to walk into new daycares and schools alone without a backward glance.

Do I want to puncture that ease? Didn't I in fact work hard to give her this refuge? Do I want to contaminate or prescript her world prematurely by telling her that there are people who would despise her just because of who her parents are, or because of the way she looks? Do I want to tell her the queasy fact that derision can wear the face of desire? Am I being irresponsible or cowardly by not telling her? Or are such warnings pointless because no amount of being told something like this can approximate the unexpected violence of such an experience?

Did I not dream of a world where she is not divided from her own body?

6.

My daughter was born on Mischief Night, the night before Halloween. So October is always a big month for us. When they were small, every August in anticipation of Halloween and before my school semester starts, my kids and I would gather to discuss and plan their Halloween costumes. I treasured these planning sessions because it was *our* project and because I got glimpses into how they saw themselves. I think children love dress-up, not for disguise or escape, the way it often is for adults, but because it is an exercise in possibility, a rehearsal for what they could be or imagine they already are. As they got older, my daughter started helping out and then taking over the sewing: a fine-boned Victorian gown after she read *Pride and Prejudice;* a demon slayer from some anime who carried a life-size boomerang that she crafted out of papier-mâché; a mythic warrior wielding a mask of Medusa.

Unlike me, my daughter the seamstress is not limited by ready-made patterns or even by materials. She thinks anything is possible. When she was seventeen, she wanted to make a costume despite the pandemic and the quarantine. She had been reading the Arthurian legend and decided to reimagine what Uther Pendragon would have been like had he been a woman. I found her at the kitchen table making a list of her own: bevor, cuirass, rerebrace, plackart, pauldron, gauntlet, cuisse, greaves, and sabatons . . . a litany of armorial bearings. She bound her body with rolls of duct tape, making a mummy of herself, on top of which she drew the segmented suit. She then cut herself out of that second skin, pieces of which became the base patterns for the armor she fashioned out of foam boards, cloth, and pieces of plastic she found in her dad's workshop that she heated up and molded.

Weeks after that Halloween, I found in the corner of her room the discarded duct tape husks, hollow but still holding the shape of her slim torso, arms, and legs. I thought about her going off to college next year, which means leaving behind the shelter of love that so far has been hers for the taking. I thought about the beauty of new shells and the emergence of new vulnerabilities. She will soon have to see—or might already be seeing—her body as a thing-in-the-world. Has she been crafting armors or extensions?

The word *blazon* comes from the French for "coat of arms" or "shield" and describes a lineage of heraldry. But in literature it alludes to a type of poem, a poetic device in which the (usually female) body is dissected and cataloged. For men, a blazon is a legacy; for women, a condition of fragmentation. I hope fervently, against all that I know, that my daughter will continue to fashion for herself all that is possible in a broken world.

7

Things Not to Do to My Daughter When I'm Old

When you are old and gray and full of sleep, take this down and read. And heed.

1. Do not start counting down the days left in her visit on the day she arrives.
2. Do not make it hard to help you.
3. Do not call her every day; let her call as she needs.
4. Do not itemize your ailments when speaking with her. (Remember: This backfires. It will alienate more than it draws.)
5. Do not let her know your fears when she's living her life. (Just like when you forced yourself to relax and touch the snake and the worm in the backyard when she was little so as not to instill fear in her, you must contain your clenched panic when she declares she's spending six months halfway across the world. Focus on the memory of how proud you were when she would go out in the yard with her yellow booties to collect worms after a rain.)

6. Do not ask if she is dressed warmly enough. And never ask, if she has children, whether she has dressed them warmly enough.

7. Do not send her articles about the importance of sunscreen.

8. Do not ask for tech advice unless you are willing to listen. (Take notes so you won't have to ask again.) This goes along with "Don't refuse to learn new things."

9. Do not force her to do a running self-commentary: Yes, I'm going up the stairs; yes, I'm reading; yes, I'm working on the computer.

10. Do not engage in ritualistic repetition, where you ask the same things over and over as a way to stave off your anxiety.

11. Do not do crazy things like hand-wash all the dishes, let them dry, and then put them in the dishwasher because you're afraid that wet, dirty dishes waiting in the dishwasher will attract cockroaches.

12. Do not be coy or "Chinese polite" about how you want to live your life when you can no longer live the life you want.

13. Do not lie. (Except in case of Rule #5.)

14. Do not be a defeatist. You don't have to aspire to be a spunky old lady, just don't be a sad sack.

15. Know that she may have to step away to survive.

Part III

Beauty for the Unbeautiful

8

Beauty Queen

Beauty—its judgment, care, and maintenance—made up the song of my childhood, and my lack of it a note in the background. I can't say I was the ugly duckling, because I never did turn into the swan, but I did feel like a stepchild growing up in a family of celebrated, local beauties. In the small city of Tainan, my maternal grandmother was known for two things: for being the wife of the first doctor in town trained in Western medicine, and for her classic Chinese beauty. I was sure that the reason she never went into the sun without cover and rarely smiled, certainly never in a photograph, had something to do with deeply held ideas at the back of her mind about the pale suffering beauties of classic Chinese literature. Her younger sister, Great-Aunt #4, had what people called a "Western" beauty—some unspoken Dutch ancestry back there somewhere—that earned her a premature but prestigious marriage and made her the toast of Shanghai in the 1940s, when she crossed the Taiwan Strait at age sixteen with her husband some thirty years her senior. On their wedding night, he gave her an antique, gilded Louis XIV handheld vanity mirror and matching hairbrush. To show her disinterest (in the gift, the marriage, him), she threw them deep

under the platform bed where he couldn't reach. For the rest of
their marriage, he showered her with jewels, furs, servants, and
houses decorated with Japanese gardens and Western appliances,
and she slowly learned to take pride in that.

My mother had her own kind of beauty, the kind other
women whispered about. "*That* Mei-Yin!" I could hear the
admiration and the envy in their voices. As a kid, I liked to
tease her that it was a good thing that she was indeed beautiful,
otherwise being named after beauty itself would have been terrible. (She liked that joke.) Her face had the kind of symmetry
that scientists resorted to when they tried to explain beauty, with
teeth that never needed straightening, intentional eyebrows that
didn't need filling in, and wide brown eyes. There were many
stories, like how, growing up in Tainan, she was for several years
the local high school's choice to play the Statue of Liberty in the
annual city parade. I don't know why a parade in Tainan would
have featured the Statue of Liberty, except maybe something to
do with the American liberation of Taiwan from Japanese occupation during World War II or just the general worldwide idea
in those days that America represented this much-envied beacon
of freedom. But I did ask my mom if they painted her green. She
laughed and said of course not. She stood on top of the float in
a now modest but probably then risqué green one-piece bath-
ing suit with a metal crown, a green papier-mâché torch in one
hand, and with her one free hand waved slowly to the people, in
the way of beauty queens.

Beauty was a matter of everyday practice and interest for my
mother and therefore for me as a child. What little memories I
have of my life in Taipei are concentrated around age six when
my brother, a year older than I, had started grade school. That
was the year I had my mother all to myself. In the mornings,

after she fed and saw my father and brother off, she would take me with her to the neighborhood beauty shop. I loved going to the salon with her: the blast of warm, dry air greeting my face the moment the doors opened, especially on a cold day. I even liked the slightly burned, chemically smell that permeated the space. My mother said it was vulgar to gossip with the other women, so she was mostly quiet, but I enjoyed leaning on her knees while she read magazines and I daydreamed out the steamy windows, cradled by the hums of dryers and chatter all around us.

Going to the hairdresser every day to have your hair washed and put up seems extravagant, but back then in Taipei most apartments didn't come with showers, just tubs. Washing your own hair in the kitchen sink was awkward, while hair salons were abundant and inexpensive. At the salon, I loved watching the hairdresser pull and brush out my mother's hair before twisting it and expertly pinning it up. Unlike my own wispy hair, my mother had a crazy-thick head of hair, so thick that you could barely see the scalp even as the hairdresser pulled on the hair. Afterward, we usually strolled around the shops before heading home for my mother to make lunch and prepare dinner. Looking back, I can see that these outings must have been my mother's "me time," but I thought of them as ours. Those ambles were full of pleasures and pitfalls. I loved the time alone with my mom, how relaxed she seemed, and how she would talk to me about what we saw in the shop windows. I hated the meat store on the corner with the roast ducks hanging on steel hooks, their inert heads and necks grotesquely bent, because whenever my mother was mad she would threaten to string me up like those ducks. Every time we went by that storefront, I edged her closer to the road.

I remember how self-conscious I was of my mother's long

legs, often shown to their best advantage in her miniskirts. This was at the height of the 1960s, and my mother was, of course, at the top of the fashion game. But it seemed to me back then that her dresses were terribly short, which must have seemed doubly so from my vantage point, looking up. I remember how annoyed she would be when I insisted on pulling down the side of her skirt as I walked alongside her. My gestures of modesty on her behalf probably exposed her more than they helped. But at the time I was deeply embarrassed by the lingering looks she would get from men and women alike. Then there were the dreaded boutiques that she would coax me into, the brightly lit, hip, modern shops that she liked, where they sold clothes from abroad (America, France, Japan), fully displayed on racks rather than folded inside sealed plastic bags. These shops followed the Western custom of allowing you to try on clothes right there, and often they would breach convention and hire young male salespersons. How I disliked those men, the way they stood too close to the dressing rooms, suggested items for my mom to try on, or commented on her figure. It didn't occur to me that they were simply trying to make a sale or that I was chaperoning my mother like some jealous mother-in-law. I don't know where my prudery as a child came from, but those boutique encounters made me angry at those men . . . and at my mother.

But one of my favorite and most vivid memories from child-hood is watching the annual Miss Universe contest on television with my mom, the other activity that was shared by the two of us alone and that we both looked forward to. We weren't idle watchers. We dissected the features of every contestant: how one year Miss France's eyes were so light blue that you couldn't tell if she was looking at you; how Miss Peru had a lilt to her lips that made her appear sweet-natured; how Miss Japan's legs were slim but pigeon-toed; how Miss USA looked like sunshine but her mouth was too wide. We were not fooled by trick makeup or easy glamor. We parsed the nuances, gradations, and particular qualities of beauty exhibited by each contestant. There's beauty and then there's beauty. Some beauty can be instantaneous but shallow, the kind that grabs your eyes but of which you soon tire. Some beauty can be sad, some cheap, some bold, some fine, some captivating but ferocious, like that of the actress Ann-Margret with her slightly crooked, sly smile.

The highlight of the event for us was the evening gown competition. There we really went to town: pored over every detail, cut, lines, and fabric, lamented when a particularly unfortunate choice ruined a woman's chances, were joyous when a particularly arresting creation came onstage, something that lingered on the mind, a design that *moved.* I was always glad when my mother agreed with my assessments because that meant that I, even as a child, had good taste, which my mother thought made up a great deal for the lack of something else.

The Miss Universe competitions must have taken place in the summer months, when Taipei was at its hottest and stickiest, because we would always be setting up fans in the living room in anticipation. During a commercial break, my mom would send me downstairs to the mini-mart on the first floor of our apartment building to get something cold for us. Snacks, magazines, pots and pans, toiletry items, and anything else you can imagine crowded that tiny space, filling every nook of the wall from floor to ceiling. There were displays, too, on the ground, stacked on rows of low shelves that bulged out onto the sidewalk. I would carefully pick my way to the icebox at the back of the store. My mom and I preferred either the taro pops or those single-serving ice creams whose surface you scraped with those little flat wooden spoons. Once in a while she would relent and allow me to also buy a box of these minty candies shaped like ersatz cigarettes that I liked, with tips tinted yellow like tiny flames. Now I see why my mother disapproved of that particular treat (the very idea of marketing candy to children in the guise of cigarettes!), but I loved the feeling of sophistication as I held each slim rod between my fingers the way I saw grown women do on TV.

In any event, I would spring back up the stairs, and my mother and I would settle into the couch with our treats and continue our judging. Even now, every time I see a woman in the media—on television or in a magazine—my brain immediately runs an automatic assessment: a flawed or mistaken makeup move, an infelicitous sartorial choice, a prettiness that wears thin, or an unflattering hairstyle. As an adult and a feminist, I'm horrified that I do this, and in fact the information means nothing. Yet the appraisal always happens before I can check myself.

My maternal grandmother used to say I was "all Cheng," her way of saying I didn't look like her beautiful daughter. My mother always maintained that I could've been pretty had it not been for my teeth, a terrible overbite inherited from my father's side of the family. She bemoaned this fact for most of my life, as if my teeth were the culprit to be blamed for any misfortunes that might befall me. This complaint had always made me feel bad in two ways: sad that I had let her down and a little mad that she was really saying something about my father. All through my teens and beyond, my mother repeatedly urged me to get corrective braces. I never did. I'm kind of proud of that little resistance in me. I'm not above doing what I can to improve my looks, but I don't care enough to modify actual body parts. Once, on a trip back to Taiwan when I was in my mid-twenties, my mother tricked me into visiting an old friend who turned out to be an orthodontist. After examining me, he told my mother, "She has a slight overbite, but it's normal. If she were my daughter, I wouldn't do anything about it."

Afterward, my mother walked alongside me with a frown, puzzling, "How extraordinary! I guess we have to believe him because he's the expert. But how could it be? I was just so sure you had a terrible overbite all these years." A block later, she told me casually, "You know, I had forgotten how Amah"—that is, her mother and my grandmother—"used to worry that I had an overbite, too." She with the perfect teeth? How had this never come up before? She shook her head gently and walked on without saying anything else. Now I wonder whether the reason my grandmother never smiled for the camera had less to do with her ideals about restrained beauty than with whatever imagined notions she had about her teeth. What I had taken to be her determined grace might in fact have been an anxious pose.

On that same trip, my mother and I went down south to Tainan and saw Great-Aunt #3, the one who never left Taiwan, a fact that somehow always seemed entangled with the other facts that she never married and was understood to be the unattractive sister among a cadre of beauties. She came close to give me a good, long look. She hadn't seen me since I was a small child. She peered into my face, patted my arm, and confided, "Oh, you don't know, but when you were little, you were so . . . so . . . so . . . so . . ." I thought she was going to say I was so well behaved or at least so cute. Instead, she said, "You were so . . . so . . . so . . . ugly!" That's what you get from a Taiwanese relative: brutal honesty.

As a teenager in the American South, I didn't get prettier.

In high school, I was just too different. Boys glanced, curious, but did not engage. I looked to my family: I had no Chinese beauty. I looked at my new world: I had no Western beauty. Over time, I gathered that there were some American ideas out there about the exotic "Oriental" woman, but the reality of me bore no resemblance to that. Now, as an adult, I think of myself as secretly a very plain woman, secretly because I think I've been able to hide my lack of beauty behind my sense of style. Sometimes, I look into the mirror and grin to myself, taking a wicked, gleeful pleasure at just how genuinely and actively ugly I am, marveling at how those who love me now seem not to know this truth . . . a grand deception, a magic trick.

Much as I adore my girlfriends, I don't really like going clothes shopping with anyone but my mother because we are both quick and scarily efficient about the exercise. Friends want to try on things, debate options, seek one another's opinions, but my mother and I pretty much know what will or will not look good on us at a glance. I favor clean, well-cut, fitted lines in quality fabrics, something that follows the body faithfully but not cloyingly, something so expertly cut and meticulously sewn that it looks quietly, painfully expensive even decades later. Such a thing is nothing less than sheer armor. In Taiwan and back in the day, my mother and grandmother had their own tailor who would come to the house, bearing reams of sample materials. The women would spread out around the kitchen table. Mother and Amah would bend over the textiles, parse their quality and texture, smooth and stretch, discuss ideas, draw pictures of what they envisioned, and the seamstress would make the clothes, coming back multiple times for fittings. I learned that it's best to base a design on the material; let the cloth, texture, and color lead. With any leftover material, my mother would ask the tailor to make something for me. I always wanted to have an identical dress as my mom's, but she invariably dictated: same fabric, different design. Grown-up patterns don't suit little girls, she'd say. Besides, it's much more charming to have different outfits in the same fabric than to make the mistake of being too matchy-matchy.

Once, though, my mother called for the tailor just for me. I was in the third grade and chosen to play Snow White in the school play. (This was before coming to America, when the idea of a snow-white princess—and the Statue of Liberty, for that matter—still held universal promise, even for a little Chinese girl.) I couldn't tell who was more excited, my mother or me. We told the seamstress that I needed a princess dress: not pink—too expected, too pedestrian—but perhaps something in cool blue. I still remember the design and the fabrics we finally settled on: a pale sky blue for the underdress, to be covered by a translucent, icy blue netting that overlaid the full-length gown (my first ever), and a crenate, thick, embroidered lace in a slightly lighter blue for the high-waisted bodice. The scalloped lace would be repeated below like a line of waves lapping the bottom of the skirt.

The dress floated about my ankles when I walked.

A week before the play, however, my teacher, with much embarrassment, asked me to switch roles with the girl who was supposed to play the evil stepmother and who had been unhappy with her assignment. The girl also happened to be the headmistress's daughter. I went home heartbroken, filled with shame. How do I tell my mom? She had already spent all that time and money on the fancy dress. And now I'd gone from the chosen to the unchosen, from the beloved to the despised. Instead of my pretty gown, I was going to have to wear an old

Author as a child in costume

crone's raggedy black cloak and maybe even sport an unsightly mole on my chin.

Over the years I have grieved that my mother, for all her scrupulous care of us, was not the kind of warm fuzzy mother that I wanted. She wasn't someone who talked about hurt feelings or indulged in your disappointments; she had little patience with tearful children with red, contorted faces. And I was such a sad reflection on her, not only by not being a beauty but also by not sharing her unbreakable composure. I cried too much. I had too many ugly feelings . . . too many *feelings,* period. But this time, *this* time, my mother did the unexpected. She was not impatient, nor did she reprimand me for crying. She sat down next to me where I was hunched over and said, "You know, the evil stepmother is a much better and much more important role. You get to really act instead of lying down pretending to be a dead person most of the time." But what about my pretty dress? I asked; the evil stepmother must wear an ugly cloak. Years later I can still hear in my mind's ear the certainty in my mother's voice when she replied, "You can still wear your dress under the cloak. *You* will know it's there even if other people can't see it."

Freud thought that vanity and narcissism were primarily female pathologies, that beautiful women were by nature self-absorbed and dangerous, exerting a fatal charm much like, in his words, "cats and large beasts of prey." For him, the other side of female self-gazing is the male gaze. For the Brothers Grimm, *Snow White* offered a cautionary tale about female conceit and deadly competition. The emergence of the daughter must mean the death of the mother. But a woman might tell what passes between women differently. Perhaps a story about double vision: beauty real and unreal; expectations imposed and imagined; role playing and secret freedoms; the arrival into self-sufficiency;

and the hold of old attachments. Embedded within the enmity between mothers and daughters are also love's mutual reflections: what's in the mirror vacillates, sometimes unseen, sometimes too close, to the beholder.

I have a photo that my mother took of the play.

In the photograph, I am hunched over with a snarl on my face, the poison apple in one hand. You can see the little prince, his entrance premature, pressing in from the threshold; behind him, a sliver of my teacher's face. I had just entered from stage right, slowly and diffidently, dragging one foot behind me, my body bent over. I thought I was doing a good job playing an infirm old woman, but I also secretly knew that the posture forced my cloak to gape open, letting fall the spill of icy blue tulle.

Author playing the evil stepmother in an elementary
school production of *Snow White*

9

Joan Didion Talks to Marie Kondo About Packing and Self-Respect

"... one runs away to find oneself, and finds no one at home."

—Joan Didion

1. BAGGED

I had to reread Didion's essay on self-respect from *Slouching Towards Bethlehem* several times. It's full of contradictions. Self-respect represents for Didion, in her words, a "separate peace," a "private reconciliation," but it's also something to be "developed, trained, coaxed forth." She describes it as a sense of "innate worth," yet she writes about it like something that you have to take on and perform, like an expensively tailored coat that you learn to wear casually. Self-respect is the thing she realized she lacked and needed the day she lost her confidence and had to question her own heretofore unquestioned entitlement: "The day that I did not make Phi Beta Kappa ... I lost the conviction that lights would always turn green for me, the pleasant certainty ... of the love of a good man; lost a certain touching faith in the totem power of good manners, clean hair."

But alongside being "driven back" to one's "real self-respect," an innate resource of fortitude (as she says, "in order to remember it, I must've known it"), Didion also thinks of self-respect as an intentional, outward cultivation of self-preservation, a process of fostering a sense of one's rightness even when, or especially when, you're not in the right. Self-respect is the lovely thing that allows you to sleep, avoid galling self-reviews, and accept "that anything worth having has its price." She gives the reader two disconcerting models of self-respect: the British imperialist "Chinese Gordon" extending British interests in China on the one hand and the conquest of the American West from "the Indians" on the other. She writes with a brutal, world-weary élan: "Indians were simply part of the *donné* . . . People who respect themselves are willing to accept the risks that Indians will be hostile, that the venture will go bankrupt." Having "moral nerve," after all, is not the same as having morals. This is along the lines of the injunction to "own it!" even when you have erred (as in, "So you had an affair . . . own it!"). Here, personal entitlement ("The light will always turn green for me") has been substituted by another form of entitlement ("I will make the light turn green, no matter the cost to others"). Is it blindness or insight that allows Didion to draw this coextension between Western individual self-possession and Western territorial conquest?

That's the beauty and the trouble with Didion: her insights can teeter between being either a symptom or its critique. It's not her intention, but her knife-edged, relentless observations about her surroundings and herself can offer such an exquisite study of whiteness, especially its middle-class privileges and middle-class white femininity.

For Didion, self-respect means having "character," which

means *self-restraint,* keeping the proverbial stiff upper lip. "It was once suggested to me," she wrote, "as an antidote to crying, I put my head in a paper bag . . . there is a sound physiological reason . . . but the psychological effect alone is incalculable: it is difficult in the extreme to continuing fancying oneself Cathy in *Wuthering Heights* with one's head in a Food Fair bag." Here white (British/WASPy) male stoicism translates into a bracing ban on the discombobulated woman. Didion tells us that this small act of self-discipline (and muffling) enacts a "ritual" that helps "one" (surely the woman) "remember who and what we are."

How do you stop a woman from crying like a girl? Put a bag over her head. Again Didion gives us a double-punch observation, both offering a rehearsal of gender expectation and revealing its embedded critique.

Might we ask, what is more humiliating, being caught crying or wearing a bag over your head? What does it mean to hide your failure or sorrow by concealing it behind a facade that does nothing but announce the existence of such angst? I'm reminded of this funny little book I once owned called *101 Unuseless Japanese Inventions,* which had handy life hacks such as a loud-noise button on the toilet that disguises other, more embarrassing sounds or a "chin hammock" designed to catch unsightly drool from its wearer while napping on the commuter train. Both face-saving devices seem to me to broadcast the very thing they were meant to camouflage.

Didion isn't one for displaying unnecessary baggage, literal or otherwise. In *The White Album* she famously celebrates her own efficient way of living by sharing her method on how to pack. Here's the list she kept on the door of her closet in Hollywood:

To Pack and Wear:
2 skirts
2 jerseys or leotards
1 pullover sweater
2 pair shoes
stockings
bra
nightgown
robe
slippers
cigarettes
bourbon

Bag with:
shampoo
toothbrush and paste
Basis soap
razor
deodorant
aspirin
prescriptions
Tampax
face cream
powder
baby oil

To Carry:
mohair throw
typewriter
2 legal pads
pens

files
house key

This list has been printed and reproduced many times in women's magazines, including *Vogue* and *Vanity Fair*, as if we could and should all pack like Joan Didion.

According to Didion, this is everything she needs when she sets out on a writing assignment. The list "enabled [her] to pack, without thinking, for any piece [she] was likely to do." Much more than practical advice, her list is the very embodiment of Didion ease: her celebrated mobility, freedom, and capacity for a cool, cosmopolitan homelessness. (Having "a leotard" and "stockings" means she "could pass on either side of the culture" . . . good advice, if your world is either the Met Gala or some underground Audrey-Hepburn-black-leotard bohemian scene.)

And, of course, Didion is too sharp-eyed not to acknowledge what's behind the list: "It should be clear that this was a list made by someone who prized control, yearned after momentum, someone determined to play her role as if she has the script, heard her cues, knew the narrative."

Yes, the key is the "as if." For someone for whom simplicity equals plenitude, which is to say, a fantasy of control, Didion nonetheless also builds into her own stratagem a conspicuous lack, a deliberate wrench in the machine. She informs us: "There is on this list one significant omission, one article I needed and never had: a watch." Of course, Didion could easily rectify this oversight and buy herself a watch. If she can carry a typewriter as part of her packing economy, then a watch is hardly too weighty. But she does not.

We discover why:

I needed a watch not during the day . . . but at night, in the motel. Quite often I would ask the desk for the time every half hour or so, until finally, embarrassed to ask again, I would call Los Angeles and ask my husband. In other words, I had skirts, jerseys, leotards . . . files and a house key, but I didn't know what time it was.

Every half hour or so? Is this a version of a reverse, self suicide check?

For someone so invested in a vision of herself as untethered—she can pick up and go anywhere, anytime—and so at ease in the world that she can "pass" everywhere, this is a shocking revelation of anxiety, dislocation, and homesickness. This little act of undermining herself—putting herself in a position of neediness, staging for herself a mise en abyme of temporal and emotional misplacement—also guarantees her company, a lifeline.

This is the bag over the head yelling for help. Or, more accurately, this is the bag placed over the head in order to stage a witness (the hotel clerk, her husband) for its silent call. This is Didion's own controlled game of loss and retrieval, her *fort-da*.

2. An Economy of Being

Careful readers of *Walden* might notice that Henry David Thoreau, for all his preaching about the necessity of sparseness, was prone to list making, the near-compulsive tallying and accretion of details, from bags of nails to ounces of flour. As in Didion, the telegraphed control is intense, extensive, self-congratulating, and self-defeating. Like Didion, he implied that what you own and carry with you says a lot about who and what you are. In the section entitled "Economy," Thoreau asks us to change the

American ethos and the American house by changing ourselves, by putting ourselves in order.

Does it seem odd that this wisdom comes to us today by way of popular culture mostly in the voice of a petite Japanese woman? Marie Kondo, Japanese lifestyle sensei of the twenty-first century, could be channeling Thoreau when she tells us, "Tidying is the act of confronting yourself; cleaning is the act of confronting nature" or "Life truly begins only after you have put your house in order."

Did Kondo steal from Thoreau or did Thoreau steal from Japanese philosophy? Scholars have long noted the intimacy between American Transcendentalism and Eastern ideas and religions from Buddhism to Confucianism to Daoism. Writers like Thoreau and Ralph Waldo Emerson were enamored of Asian philosophies and religions, and both felt they discovered "Asia" in their own Transcendentalist views of nature and human ethics. At the same time, lesser known but also documented is the fact that the works of Thoreau and Emerson were widely read by Japanese intellectuals during the Meiji and Taishō periods (1868–1926). Nineteenth-century American Orientalism riding the wave of transglobal capitalism was more of a two-way street, a more knotted exchange of transnational ideas than would first appear.

But one thing we can say for sure, Kondo draws from that entanglement of American ideas of modernity (clean minimalism) and ancient Eastern philosophy, just as she taps into some very deep-seated Western notions about Japanese spareness and refinement. We can talk about Modernist Orientalism just as easily as Modernist Primitivism. This is where drawing finer nuances within the discursive practice of Orientalism can be instructive: where Chineseness has long connoted extravagant

and decadent ornamentality for the West, Japaneseness connotes simplicity and organicity. Both are Western inventions,
but this is why modernists from Roland Barthes to Le Corbusier
could say they were fascinated by Japan but held no interest in
China.

Spareness = neatness = cleanliness = moral uprightness.

It's revealing that the message of "less is more" in our age of
overconsumption and capitalist overdrive would be more palat-
able, more appealing, and more *natural* when coming from a
neat, diminutive Japanese woman ventriloquizing ancient Eastern aesthetics and theology. Kondo's strategy for dealing with
the threat of being swallowed up by things, even as one might be
shopping for a second house, carries a heavy dose of mysticism:
"I sometimes think that all houses must be connected by some
kind of network. It's as if, when you tidy your house properly,
your house announces to the network that you take good care
of your home, and this attracts another to you." Here we see a
materialism so intense and well honed that it emerges as a form
of spiritualism.

In her television series *Tidying Up with Marie Kondo,* Kondo,
upon entering the Western homes of her usually American clients, would always begin by bowing down. She "greets" and
"connects" with the house, as if she were entering an ancient
Shinto shrine. The camera would track the startled expressions
of the clients, at once charmed and mystified by such a quaint
master and her equally exotic rituals. When you let Marie Kondo
into your house, you'd better be prepared to say good-byes, but
you get Beauty and Inner Peace in return for your renunciations.

"Konmari," as Marie Kondo likes to call herself (even her
name is foldable!), thus offers the Western audience a promise
of spiritual peace grounded in the management of the mate-

rial. In this way, her very domestic practice is not unlike the corporate Zen culture that has infused American businesses in the twenty-first century, the way American corporate culture borrows from touches of Zen Buddhism to inure its workers to the demands of endless work hours, be it "mindfulness" sessions in the conference room or "nap pods" at Google headquarters. The enormous appeal of Marie Kondo for our neoliberal age is this combination of spirituality and thingness, of spirituality *in* thingness. Her carefully crafted domiciles dovetail neatly into a network of saturated capitalism and corporate management. Her brand of Eastern philosophy and religion, or at least their guises, lubricate the dysphorias, the messiness, of Western capitalism. For all the smallness of her modest domains (clothes, books, *komono*/miscellany), Kondo brings all the force and aesthetic and emotional power of the centuries-old utopian fantasy of "Eastern simplicity" to a world overwhelmed by things.

Anyone who has ever felt the urge to be organized knows that it exacts a great deal of continual labor, but here's the beauty of the Kondo method: it elevates the drudgery of cleaning up and the unglamorous chore of organizing to the level of aesthetic practice and to the status of Virtue, even Ethical Necessity. Kondo writes in her book *Spark Joy,* "Life truly begins only after you have put your house in order . . . [and] honed your decision-making . . . A joyful home is like your own art museum." Kondo sells a program that is also a theology, a state of mind, and, most importantly, the assurance of a *curated* life.

Kondo insists, "Taking good care of your things leads to taking good care of yourself." In short, self-respect.

Suddenly, we are back in the territory of Joan Didion. These two women—their affects, their styles, their social zeitgeists, their racial and national origins—could not be more different.

Yet both circle the territory of female efficiency and control. Both worry about the female body being leaky and messy. Not surprisingly, Kondo has packing tips, too. Her counsel to "pack drawers like a Japanese bento box," "fold clothes like origami," and learn the proper order of packing a suitcase promises, like Didion's list, self-sufficiency, pragmatic efficiency, usefulness, style, and the joy of a job well done. (Claire Wilcox, writer and senior curator of fashion at the Victoria and Albert Museum, once noted that the kimono is the ideal item of clothing to fold and pack because, unlike Western clothes that are built around the body, the kimono is purportedly structured two-dimensionally, as if Japaneseness itself were structurally placid, unperturbed by human disarray.) For all of her celebration of the organic, Kondo herself rehearses the trope of Asiatic robot-icness when she offers her one, repeated, best advice on how to succeed as a good packer: "The key is to pretend you are a robot and move quickly and efficiently." Don't let your emotions get the better of you on your way to joy!

I can't help but remember that Didion defined self-respect as "the ability to discriminate, to love and to remain indifferent," as if the last two could coexist. The fantasy here is one of control, of self-curation, of proper things (even of loss) in proper places: "To assign unanswered letters their proper weight, to free us from the expectations of others, to give us back to ourselves . . . the great, the singular power of self-respect." We can start to see how certain discourse of female self-determination, while grant-ing power, can also impose an ideal of order that would not leave much room for disorder, which is to say, life.

Kondo's exhortation (again, surely to women) to "clear your mind, allow new projects, save time," her instructions for tam-ing the odd-shaped clothing item by forcing it back into a foldable "rectangle," her equation of self-care with self-discipline ("the ability to . . . spark joy . . . [is] the ability to decide where to keep each thing you choose and *always put it back in its place*"; my emphasis) are all but aestheticized versions of the prescription to pack your face away in a paper bag: an *art* of self-management.

It is Jia Tolentino, hailed as the Joan Didion of our times, who points out that the rhetoric of female self-care has grown into an overwhelming and killing discourse for women about "self-optimization." She describes this version of the ideal woman: "Everything about this woman has been preemptively controlled to the point that she can afford the impression of spontaneity and, more important, the sensation of it—having worked to rid her life of artificial obstacles, she often feels legitimately care-free." The worst thing about this scripted life is that it grants the illusion and *feeling* of agency; after all, the woman can see herself as the architect of this project of constant self-improvement.

Tolentino's habitual "chopped-salad eater" could have been a disciple from the Konmari school: "The ritualization and neatness of this process . . . obscure the intense, circular artifice that defines the type of life it's meant to fit into." Here Tolentino refers to the fast-food salad chain called Sweetgreen and its Taylorist-fashioned food and service line, but the salad-store-as-metaphor also registers exactly its threefold attraction: the triple optimization of calorie reduction, time reduction, and self-reduction. Self-care, self-respect, and self-pruning have become the new imperatives for the ideal woman and ideal life.

Looking back on Didion, I find myself grateful for her little act of self-sabotage, her one remembered omission. In her essay, she writes about the virtue of self-respect as a form of ownership, of possessing the ultimate property: yourself. (Otherwise, one is liable to "find no one home!") But, at the end of the essay, by inserting the lack that is the absent watch, she makes room for dispossession, uncertainty, messiness, relationality . . . for *need* to disrupt the closed circuit of the well-packed woman.

10

"American Girl"

The young woman behind the glossy pink counter asked whether I wanted a facial, a wash, and a blowout. It took me a few beats to realize that the services were meant not for me but for my daughter's eighteen-inch doll. A quick check of the price list behind the salesperson's head—$45 for facial; $65 for wash and style; $18 for ear piercing—had not immediately helped to clarify the situation.

My daughter was seven, and we were standing in the flagship store of the American Girl brand on prime Manhattan real estate: a teeming seven-level megastore on Fifth Avenue with ever-winding escalators, gleaming cases, a full-service café, and the aforementioned beauty salon. We were in doll-land, where real women and real girls get to enjoy their real economic and girly privileges properly: through their dolls. How clever it would have been for this temple of capitalism and American femininity to offer its clientele of exhausted mothers a little respite of self-pampering for themselves. I think that was a missed business opportunity for the American Girl Corporation. But then I should have realized that the objects of care at American Girl store were neither the mothers nor the little girls, but the dolls themselves.

My brother, who has two sons and no daughters of his own, had given my daughter this indulgent gift of an American Girl doll just a year prior. I hadn't heard about the doll at the time and didn't know that it was such a coveted object. At a whopping $100+ a pop even back then, this toy would not have found its way into my home but for my brother's generosity. The doll seemed to have brought with it its own social entrée. An invitation arrived from one of my daughter's classmates to invite us, along with my daughter's doll, to a birthday party at the American Girl Café. I didn't know how the birthday girl knew that my daughter owned an American Girl doll. Perhaps they talked about it at school; perhaps it was simply the assumption of our upper-middle-class town. On arrival at the restaurant in the Manhattan store, we found next to every child's seat a miniature, perfectly doll-size high chair accompanied by its own miniature place settings. The dolls were to sit and dine with the girls, of course.

Unlike the Barbie doll, which was based on the German high-class call girl Bild Lilli, a cartoon character and then toy used as a gentleman's gag gift from the 1940s, the American Girl doll celebrated American wholesomeness, innocent girlhood, and realism—that is, as real as dolls can get. Each doll comes with a name, a biography, and a booklet detailing her story. My daughter's doll, Felicity Merriman, described as "spunky and spirited," lived in pre-Revolutionary colonial Williamsburg, Virginia, in 1774. She had sparkling green eyes that opened and closed, long auburn hair, a "huggable" cloth body, and a movable head and limbs of smooth vinyl. She wore what the Pleasant Company, original maker of the American Girl, described as an "authentic" 1770s-style outfit: a "traditional" floral patterned blue-and-yellow dress with a scoop neck, short sleeves with ribbon detail, bustling in the back, and an attached contrast petticoat, white knee-high stockings, and "sturdy brown shoes" with golden decorative buckles. (I especially liked the emphasis on the "sturdy" shoes. None of that frivolous Mattel nonsense about impossibly tiny, squishable high heels, mind you!) The booklet that Felicity came with was entitled *Love and Loyalty.*

To say that dolls reinforce gender roles is both obvious and an understatement. Dolls play such a commonplace yet complex psychocultural role. They are imitations, ideals, surrogates, prosthetics, and projections: offering young girls mirrors for self-, maternal, and social identification. They present idealized cuteness, and they reflect their owners' aspiring cuteness. They serve as a kind of pet, training you in the mimicry of care but more forgiving than a real animal if you are a forgetful caretaker. Dolls make pets out of their owners, too, for both dolls and pets allow their owners to participate in this weird twinning of dominance and nurture. If the pet can be seen as an emotional laborer tasked with making those in power feel better about themselves, then we might also think about the emotional labors that little girls are expected to perform for adults, and in return receive protection and cherished care.

There's a reason why cute things tend to be small, rounded, and malleable; they invite emotional responses that seem both to overwhelm the adult (the *aawwww* factor) and to draw out an intensity that can border on violence. Cute things ask to be petted, pitied, and squeezed, to sink your fingers in, and even to bite. The cultural theorist Sianne Ngai has observed that there is an intimacy between cuteness and vulnerability, suggesting in fact that the latter preconditions the former. It's a short stop from vulnerability to pity and injury. Psychologists today have even coined a phrase, "cute aggression," to describe the ways in which our responses to the cute can carry a tinge of assault. The Japanese artist Yoshitomo Nara, pop-cultural king of the *kawaii*, puts his fingers on this uneasy affinity between cuteness, injury, and aggression with his haunting, plastinated images of endlessly cute children: wide-eyed innocents that look strangely blank and hollow; a placidly calm child wielding a knife; a child dressed like a kitten riding atop a slightly too-small melamine ducky in an act of both sweet play and sly subjection (Figure 9). (Who's the pet here?)

It's as if Nara's children have both internalized and projected back against the adult viewers their insistent demand for piercing and pierced cuteness.

In her novel *Nightwood*, Djuna Barnes says this chilling thing about dolls and womanhood: "We give death to a child when we give it a doll—it's the effigy and the shroud." Freud names dolls as a key trigger for the uncanny. The psychoanalysts Nicolas Abraham and Mária Török describe the ego as having layers of spectral shells, not unlike a Russian nesting doll. Reading all this, I think womanhood is itself a kind of serial encasement, or entombment: layers that are alternately formative, protective, and restrictive.

It seems revealing that the nesting doll—should we call it an "it" or a "they," since the matryoshka is both split and multiple?—represents an idealized life cycle of womanhood, from the outward maternal casing to the innermost "baby" inside, a progression that is also a regression. And as a brilliant graduate student of mine once said to me about the matryoshka, there's not a lot of space for a room of one's own when you are one of these instances.

Dolls do not only bring a kind of gendered claustrophobia; they also carry deep racial scars in American history. I am thinking of the famous "doll tests" that played such a critical role in *Brown v. Board of Education* (1954), arguably the most momentous Supreme Court ruling in U.S. history. In the years leading up to *Brown*, activists and civil rights lawyers had challenged segregation but had repeatedly found it nearly impossible to overturn *Plessy v. Ferguson* (1896), which upheld Jim Crow laws through the principle of "separate but equal." When Thurgood Marshall came into the picture, he knew he had to prove that "separate is *inherently* unequal," but how? Then he came across the works of the social psychologists Kenneth and Mamie Clark. In the 1930s and '40s, the Clarks conducted a series of experiments with African American children. They bought two dolls, one white, one brown, from the local dime store and showed them to the young children with whom they were working. In interview after interview, when given the choice, the majority of the African American children, including three-year-olds, found the brown dolls to be "bad" and preferred instead to play with the "good," white dolls. Several of the children went on to identify the white dolls as the ones "most like themselves," a drama of mis- and overidentification. The kids not only displayed an awareness of racial difference but also appeared to have processed the symbolic values of that difference: that white dolls connote "whiteness" and that whiteness connotes security and praise.

According to Kenneth Clark himself, what was most difficult

"Doll Test, Harlem, New York," Gordon Parks, 1947
(Courtesy of and copyright © The Gordon Parks Foundation)

for him and the other adults to witness was in fact the depth of these children's understanding:

> We were really disturbed by our findings . . . and we sat on them for a number of years . . . Some of these children . . . were reduced to crying when presented with the dolls and asked to identify with them. They looked at me as if I were the devil for putting them in this predicament. Let me tell you, it was a traumatic experience for me as well.

Psychological damage was and still is enormously difficult to prove in the courts. When Marshall first brought Kenneth Clark to introduce him to his legal team, the other NAACP lawyers were skeptical; a few made bad jokes about grown men playing with dolls. But the doll test became the evidence that changed the tide, its significance directly cited by the opinion of the Court. The doll experiment not only turned out to be the key evidence in *Brown v. Board* but also became the template for versions of and a series of psychological experiments about racial stereotypes in the field of psychology to this day.

In 1970, Toni Morrison revisited this drama in her iconic novel *The Bluest Eye,* where Claudia, one of the young girl protagonists in the novel, dismembers the blond, blue-eyed dolls given to her every Christmas by her African American mother, grandmother, and aunts. Five years later, in her equally iconic *The Woman Warrior,* Maxine Hong Kingston depicts a scene in which her child narrator stands in a deserted school bathroom physically abusing another Asian American girl, who reminds her of herself. Thus more than twenty years after Kenneth Clark testified in the Supreme Court that "this type of [racial] wound stays raw for a lifetime," it would seem that the "wound" endures, not only in the individual psyche but in the American national psyche as well, inherited across time and even across racial groups.

China dolls, geishas, slave girls . . . the myth (and the hurt) lives on. Today, even as anti-Asian sentiments rage across our country and abroad, the American pursuit of cute Asian things, including people, reaches a new height. From the inner-city status symbol of acquiring an Asian girlfriend to the suburban pleasure of Hello Kitty and chewy bobas in every mall, Americans cannot seem to get enough of Asian cuteness even as violence against persons of Asian descent, especially women, storms on. I think of Asian cuteness as an extension of the model minority myth: how Asians get to become digestible in American popular culture by becoming harmless and consumable.

The sight of Asian American female anger is rare on the national stage, and when it is visible, it is short-lived, either in the form of self-hatred (for example, the Tiger Mom) or in the guise of something commodified, diminutive, cutified, toothless. Remember the all-too-cute Angry Little Asian Girl created by Lela Lee in the 1990s (Figure 10)?

The Angry Little Asian Girl has been angry for decades without ever having created so much as a frown on the American social consciousness, even as her charming grumpiness gains widespread brand recognition (in cartoons, books, memes).

Once, in the early 1990s, someone at a dinner party told me she believed that the American Girl brand was started by an Asian American woman. I found the idea both preposterous and strangely believable, for was not the American Girl, with her fetishized Americana and her complete unawareness of anything

Asian or Asian American, exactly what a model minority might create? For Asian Americans, there are so many entrepreneurial opportunities in the art of self-erasure.

That tidbit about the originator of American Girl turned out not to be true. The American Girl was invented by precisely whom you might have suspected, a platinum-headed woman named Pleasant Rowland from Chicago. But for a moment, the fantasy of this invisible Asian American creator hidden behind the soul of the all-American Girl gripped me.

If the trope of the eroticized "China doll" seems to exist on a wholly different plane than the American Girl with her bright childhood innocence or the dark story of American racialization as in the Clark dolls, it is because yellow girlhood has never been an American option, much less a choice.

The road to the politics of beauty and its political corrections has been paved with injurious good intentions. We can see versions of the Clark experiment in the American toy market. In the 1980s, Mattel decided to offer a Black Barbie. The giant toymaker almost went bankrupt after realizing that, back then, no one, not even African Americans, wanted anything but the blond-haired, blue-eyed Barbie. (The first "Black Barbie," we should note, looked exactly like the original Barbie, except for the color of her plastic skin.) Things are different today . . . or are they? There's now more of a market for the Black Barbie and the Hawaiian Barbie, though their sales are still nowhere as robust as the original. Greta Gerwig's 2023 film *Barbie* populated the stage with alternative Barbies: fat, pregnant, Black, Asian. Yet everyone in the audience knows who the *real* Barbie is. For all the film's intentions to subvert or critique the sexist legacy of the doll, it remained deeply attached to Barbie/Margot Robbie's glossy beauty. The question of multicultural representation has continued to dog the toymaker. In 2021, Mattel decided to offer a special, commemorative Tokyo Olympics Barbie playset, boasting of an international, diverse ensemble. Unfortunately, Mattel's "Olympic Games Tokyo 2020" set didn't include an Asian doll.

After the Pleasant Company sold its American Girl brand to Mattel in 1998 for $700 million, the latter introduced in 2007 Ivy Ling, a "Best Friend" doll, who was soon "retired." (I hope I'm not the only one who hears the dysphoric echo of *Blade Runner* here.) In response to Asian American protest, in 2020, in the midst of Covid-19 and anti-Asian outbreak, the company introduced Corinne Tan, the first Asian American American Girl Doll of the Year. Corinne's story, solicited from the Asian American writer Wendy Shang, deals with her mom's remarrying a white man after her parents' divorce, and discusses her Chinese heritage and the rise in anti-Asian sentiments.

This is progress, right? Part of my continued consternation has to do with my own cynicism and what history has shown me: that multiculturalism is most welcomed when it serves as a vehicle for capitalism, and that a positive image meant to rectify a negative image can often generate its own congealment. The importance of beauty—understood as mainstream, dominant notions of beauty, which is to say white female beauty standards—continues to drive those most oppressed by it, even those who believe they are fighting that ideal by accessing that beauty for themselves. In the 1950s, one can find in the Harlem weekly *Amsterdam News* advertisements for skin-whitening creams that spelled out without reservation the racial logic of beauty: "Be Whiter, Be Better, Be Loved." The fortune of one of the first African American millionaires in America, Madame C. J. Walker, née Sarah Breedlove, was made in Black hair

straighteners and skin-lightening cream. Today, under more san-
itized guises, products such as lightening creams (now touted as
promoting health benefits) and hair straighteners continue to be
profitable, both domestically and internationally. Statistics have
shown that the most popular aesthetic surgery procedures today
for women in America, Africa, and Asia involve some form of
"ethnic corrections."

What is the other side of that correction? What does "ethnic
authenticity" look like? What does it mean to recognize ourselves in our dolls? The search for racial or ethnic authenticity
generates its own problems. In the mid-1990s, the white fashion world celebrated a twenty-one-year-old Sudanese model
named Alek Wek and congratulated itself on being progressive
by featuring a model with dark skin and reputed "authentic
African features" whom they loved to show in leopard prints.
A. Magazine, a then "hip" Asian American periodical, jauntily
announced "the end of Asian female fetishization in the porno-
graphic industry" by pointing out that Asian women were now
enjoying "stardom," rather than anonymity, in that profession.
In 2022, a Columbia professor of psychiatry notoriously tweeted
this statement about Nyakim Gatwech, a model of South Sudanese descent: "Whether a work of art or freak of nature she's a
beautiful sight to behold." From Josephine Baker to Grace Jones
to Rihanna, we have always known that "beauty" and "authenticity" skirt the edges of the fetishization and stereotyping that
they might have been meant to dispel in the first place.

Feminists have long critiqued and rejected beauty as a tool for
patriarchal control, and it is easy to see how harmful beauty and
beauty ideals can be. But that rejection is vexed for the woman
of color, a figure historically and violently excluded from the
realms of beauty or aesthetics, for whom beauty can be a source

of affirmation and redemption. It's no small thing for a woman of color to experience herself as beautiful, *even as* it remains clear to her that the very prospect of a "beautiful woman of color" would be complicit with gender stereotypes. The history of beauty, as it intersects with race, has been a messy, recurring drama of denigration and longing, wounding and idealization, self-rejection and self-affirmation.

In 2023, Mattel released the "Barbie Lunar New Year" doll, an Asian doll with clothes designed by the Chinese couturier Guo Pei, who is known for her extravagant, ornamental creations. Lunar Barbie is dressed in, in Mattel's words, "classic Chinese royal blue" with a proverbial golden dragon stitched prominently across her outfit. Is this brand-new "China doll"—this "dragon lady"—a spokesperson for new American multiculturalism or good old-fashioned American Orientalism?

11

Asian Woman Is/Not Robot

Recently *The New Yorker* published a piece that announced, "Where the Future Is Asian, and the Asians Are Robots." This belated revelation is playing catch-up to centuries of Euro-American ideas about the robotic Asian, from the notion of the insensate, mechanical "Chinese coolie" in the nineteenth century to the image of the white-collar, efficient, but uncreative Asian/Asian American office drones of the twenty and twenty-first centuries, not to mention the drove of Asian cyborgs in cyberpunk fiction. How did this idea of Asian roboticness come about? How is it that Asia, so frequently seen as antiquated, comes to represent the West's imagined technological future? From Ridley Scott's *Blade Runner* (Figure 11) to Alex Garland's *Ex Machina* (Figure 12) to Rupert Sanders's live-action remake of the Japanese anime *Ghost in the Shell* (Figure 13) and many more, there is a long line of contemporary cinematic cyberfiction in which we find "Asia" as the landscape and background for dystopic, Euro-American futures. In Disney's animated film *Big Hero 6,* San Francisco has simply become San Fransokyo.

Even more noticeable is how often the figure of the eroticized and often murderous androids in these futuristic fantasies comes in the shape of Asiatic femininity. After all, it's not far to go from "doll" to "cyborg."

We find this trope of the cybernetic courtesan on the fashion runway as well. In an arresting image that the photographer Nick Knight made for Alexander McQueen in 1997, we are given the Japanese model Devon Aoki as a "futuristic geisha." In this image, Aoki wears a lush, kimono-inspired, high-cowled, pink cherry-blossom-imprinted silk brocade, her hair cleanly swept up and elaborately sectioned off into three buns reminiscent of Shimada-style wigs. Her pale face, pink-stained cheeks, and cherry-red lips contrast with her one startlingly blue "mechanical eye," made preternatural by an opaque contact lens (a sign of sightless or ultra-sightful?). On her smooth forehead, a safety pin entwined with cherry blossoms seamlessly pierces the skin: no blood, no pain. This beauty is fashioned out of flesh and machine, skin and silk. Knight's image draws from centuries of enduring Western association of the Asiatic woman endowed with so much excessive, synthetic ornamentality that she is practically a *thing* herself. That is, "she" is so ornamental as to *be* the ornament.

In the face of this persistent visual trope, we must ask: What is the role of race—especially the "yellow race" and the "yellow woman"—in our fascination with and fear of artificial life?

Scholars use the term "techno-Orientalism" to name this preponderance of Orientalist motifs in science fiction: an extensive imagining of Asia and Asians in hyper-technological terms in popular literary, cinematic, and new media representations. But the story of the Artificial Asian Woman is much older and more profound than we think. When we say "technology" today, we think "high tech," but "personhood" (who or what counts as a person) is itself a form of technology, a language and a set of codes. And the technology of Western personhood has tangled with the language of race, gender, and inanimate matter since before the Age of Exploration through the Industrial Revolution, which is also to say, since the beginning of Western imperialism and conquests.

The idea of Asia as a threatening but alluring source of technology existed well before twentieth-century digital culture, especially if we think of *techné* in the older sense of referring to art, craft, technique, and skill. Out of the era of the China Trade and Atlantic slavery, and their aftermath, there emerged these hybrid figures who are both human and inhuman, of the flesh and not. I am thinking of those philosophic and material entanglements between Western ideas of the racial "Other" whose fleshliness seemed to blend into a thingliness capable of being used. The most egregious example is, of course, chattel slavery, where a person got made into a thing, became a tool or property, not unlike a piece of furniture. But we can also think about a history of the seductive animation of inorganic things, particularly of how a Western, imperial, racial imaginary began to infuse ornamental things with qualities imagined to belong to "Oriental" persons, and specifically "Oriental" women. The history of racism is not just about turning people into things but also turning things into persons.

One of the most arresting examples of this conflation emerges from the European discovery of Chinese porcelain, a "new" technology and material that enthralled Europe. Ever since the Portuguese first brought Chinese ceramics back to Europe in the sixteenth century and for the next three hundred years or so, this "white gold" has preoccupied European material commerce, social culture, and racial imagination. Historians of material culture have documented the impact of Chinese porcelain for the West: its importance in early global imperial trade; its role in spurring European technological invention and decorative design; and its impact on growing economic, social, and cultural values in Denmark, Germany, and France, as well as in England and its American colonies. (Our own George Washington, by the way, staked his own social status on his extensive and meticulously documented collection of fine Chinese porcelain.)

Since it took a long time before Europe could properly produce porcelain of similar quality to China's true *kaolin,* Chinese porcelain became a source of European yearning and envy, and eventually an economic threat. In the nineteenth century, when Britain and its American colonies discovered that their desires for Chinese goods, from porcelain to tea to silk, far exceeded what China wanted in return (the only thing the Qing government wanted from the West was silver), the Western powers cast about for a solution. To offset this trade imbalance, the East India Company and other British merchants started to smuggle massive amounts of opium into China illegally.

Moreover, this history of material obsession reveals how objects and materials can come to project racial meaning onto people. Scholars of material culture have documented how in the eighteenth and nineteenth centuries material substances spurred chemical experiments with colors that not only fed artisanal and industrial innovations across centuries but also promoted racial ideas. Mahogany's red sheen, glossy black lacquer, and the brilliant colors of indigo, cochineal dyes, and silver ore all carried and produced racial meanings. Race-making in the nineteenth century was thus as much an *artisanal* project as a pseudo-biological venture.

Prized for its alchemical and seemingly impossible properties, Chinese porcelain was known not only for its glossy beauty, pre-

carious refinement, and receptivity to color and design manipulation but also for its surprising durability, its miraculous
capacity to sustain the extreme high heat that lends it its translucency. These sensorial and affective values of porcelain then got
transcribed or projected onto the racialized bodies from whom
the commodities came, especially the bodies of Chinese women.
Translucent porcelain came to connote both hardness and plasticity, Old World beauty and New World technology, fragile
daintiness and insensate coolness: a mixture of antithetical symbolic meanings that are then ascribed to—indeed, *became*—the
very "stuff" of Asiatic femininity. (See Figures 14 and 15.)

You don't need a real Chinese woman to be present to achieve
her full, sensorial affect: "she" can be invoked by the flick of a
fan, the swish of silk, the swerve of a dragon, the cool curves of
poreless ceramic. This by now trite association of Asiatic female
skin with porcelain, from the enduring cliché of the pearlized
skin of Asian women capitalized on by the pharma-cosmetic
industry today to the widespread, contemporary fascination
for K-Beauty, carries this profound and layered history of an
imaginative merging of "Oriental flesh" and ornamental matter:
Chinese female flesh as porcelain; porcelain as Chinese female flesh.

The dream of the "yellow woman" has thus long been a dream
about artificial life. She has been embroiled with the synthetic
and the inhuman well before the threat of the modern machine.
In this way, she is an, if not *the,* original cyborg.

As the early Western romance with china/China started
to sour when Euro-American acquisitiveness began to run
in excess of what it could offer China in return, the romance
with "Chinese women" also deteriorated. In the nineteenth
century, Chinese women went from being "celestial beings" to
the "yellow peril." In 1966, *The New York Times* had this to say

about the Chinese women's gymnastics team at the Summer Olympics: "The Chinese remain the world's most erratic top gymnasts, and today, like many a Ming vase, their routines looked lovely but had cracks in several places." Not surprisingly, a similar fate of going from adulation to denigration befell Chinese porcelain: Chinese ceramics devolved in Western cultural imagination from the status of treasure to tacky crockery, with the proverbial Ming vase being the epitome of that ambivalence, both the valued antique and the outdated tchotchka.

The trope of the robotic, prosthetic yellow woman that we find in today's cinema is therefore an extension of this enduring history. One of the many consequences of this view of the Asian woman as thing is that "she/it" can be easily invoked, animated, and *borrowed*. In Garland's *Ex Machina*, the AI Ava (played by the white actress Alicia Vikander) can be seen at the end of the movie, in a gambit for freedom, peeling off the skin of her Asian "sister" to plaster on herself in a feat of extraordinary racial appropriation. (See Figures 16 and 17.) Can there be a more explicit dramatization of the sartorial uses of yellow skin?

Even when the female cyborg in cyberpunk fiction is white-presenting, she is often revealed to be "really" Asian. We see this in Rupert's *Ghost in the Shell*. There Rupert casts Scarlett Johansson to play the protagonist Major Motoko Kusanagi, a highly skilled squad leader in a fictional division of the real Japanese National Public Safety Commission. While the audience knows that the Major is an android from the get-go, by the end of the movie we discover that there's a little kernel of a human brain and soul inside her: the brain, in fact, of a young Japanese girl who was separated from her family and from most of her body and killed by the Western industrial complex that came to run Japan in this dystopian fantasy. The dead, real girl thus represents the trauma of Western Imperial capitalist presence in Japan.

So the big reveal in the plot is that this white-presenting cyborg turns out to be a Japanese girl. This paradox actually dramatizes how the Asiatic woman is almost always somehow already a machine in the Western cultural imagination. We might say that the film literalizes the insight that the Asiatic woman is the ghost within the ghost, the haunting kernel in the dream of Western modernity.

Like Knight's cherry blossom geisha with her insensate flesh, Major Kusanagi is a beauty impervious to pain. Suddenly, we see in the Asian cyborg figure the merging of two seemingly different strands of the Orientalist imagination: the "Oriental" woman as a pretty thing on the one hand and the far-from-pretty but laboring male "Chinese coolie" on the other hand. The Major-as-Johansson-as-Japanese-girl is at once pretty and instrumental, lovely but deadly, a high-tech but decorative female "coolie," if you will.

Most of all, the Major reminds us that it is racialized gender that allows the audience to both relish the Major's inhuman feats while enjoying the pity inspired by her "human condition." In other words, it is only when we discover that "she" was really Japanese that we suddenly have empathy for her as a human being. The machine only acquires humanization when sentimentalized through a *racial identification*. Racialized gender thus operates ambivalently: both as a site of inhuman objection *and* as a source for human pathos. Asiatic femininity here becomes the very source from which we seek the solace of humanity when the dream of the machine (which she also emblematizes) overwhelms us.

It is because the Asiatic woman is always already a figure of hybridity, a conflation of abstraction, matter, and corporeal fantasy, that she can represent both the Good Robot and the Bad Robot, at once a sign of futurity and of regression, the Cyborg and the Geisha.

Asian America

Part IV

12

Southern Chinese

My family first moved to Savannah, Georgia, in the early 1970s. We found a small Chinese community already there, though they were not like us. For one thing, they largely came from mainland China rather than Taiwan. For another, they all ran businesses; they were "in trade," as my mother put it. Finally, they were third- and fourth-generation Savannahians who spoke effortless English with a southern drawl. Years later I would see the comedian Henry Cho onstage, whose shtick was at least partially the unexpected, humorous dissonance of hearing perfect English with a heavy southern twang emerging out of an Asian face. But the performer sparked a recognition in me, of my own double estrangement, foreign to the white southerners and the American-born Chinese.

The Chinese in Savannah were truly ABCs, with roots in Georgia as far back as Reconstruction. My family was FOB, but FOBs with an attitude. My mother had always taken extraordinary pride in being from a highly educated family. We were descendants of poets and warriors, she would rehearse, who had lived in Tainan for centuries, since one of our ancestors defeated the Dutch in 1661 and took back the governance of what was known as Formosa. My mother insisted that we understand we were not like the Chinese laborers or the Chinese merchants that Americans were used to. Class was not about money but culture; it was about family and education, she would say. She wanted us, especially in America, to hold our heads up high.

This meant we had a curious relationship to the local southern Chinese whom we found in Savannah. We felt both a kinship and not. We got to know them but also kept our distance. It was hard anyway to break into that insular crowd, because many of them already belonged to the same two extended families: the Wus and the Chus. The generation of Wus that we knew owned the Canton Restaurant, which opened downtown in 1930 and was the first (and, for decades, the only) Chinese restaurant in town. (See Figure 18.)

The Chu family, on the other hand, opened a department store on Tybee Island in the 1930s that sold household and beach supplies. (See Figure 19.) T. S. Chu started his business by selling boiled peanuts and neckties at the beach. (The boiled peanuts I get, but the *neckties* at the beach?) Still, his business sense was unerring. He built an empire from that original business. The store is still operational today. The four sons of the Chu patriarch would go on to open ten 7-Eleven stores and mini-marts across Savannah. With the success of each son (and the eventual changes in U.S. laws), one by one they went to China and brought back a wife, each bride younger and more lovely than the previous.

When my family first arrived in Savannah, we introduced ourselves to any and as many Chinese people as we could find, even though they felt as foreign to us as the white southerners did. We went to eat at the Canton Restaurant on Sundays even though we secretly found the food disappointing. My brother and I, being snotty preteens, used to privately make fun of the dishes we would find there: moo goo gai pan (what in the world is that?), pu pu platter (that sounds like something that came out of a bathroom!), and those tasteless cookies that everyone thought were a Chinese signature. But the elderly Mrs. Wu, widow of the original owner, was always at the cash register with her huge smile. And for us, there was the undeniable pleasure of being greeted by another Chinese face.

My family had known for a year before our departure from Taipei that we were relocating to the United States. There was time for preparation, but I squandered that year away. My parents had bought us a cassette tape and a handbook to teach us the English alphabet. *A. "A" is for "Apple." [Repeat.] This is an apple. B. "B" is for "Bee." [Repeat.] This is a bee.* All of it confounded me. There was no rhyme or reason to the order of the English alphabet. I found the letters impossible to learn. Why didn't they sound like themselves once they were in words? And why *twenty-six* letters? When my brother studied, I refused. When my mother threatened me with horror stories of how far behind I would be, I countered with my favorite Chinese proverb: "I shed no tears until I see the coffin."

Well, she was right. I was up the creek when my dad put us in an American school the day after we landed in Georgia. But within a year, my brother and I were speaking English. That was the beauty of youth and the taskmaster of necessity. Within two years, our house rule went from "No Chinese in the House" to "No English in the House." First my parents worried that we wouldn't fit in; then they worried that we were assimilating too much. When I started high school, my parents decided to join the local chapter of the Georgia Chinese Benevolent Association, which has been around for almost seventy-four years.

I suspect that my parents joined the association because they wanted us to have more opportunities to be around other Asian people. Other than my brother, there were only a couple of other people of Asian descent in my private high school at the time. One of them was Mrs. Jen, our chemistry teacher, whom most students found peculiar because she spoke with a heavy Chinese accent, found no humor in their frivolity, and said things like "We can kill two stones with one bird!" but whom I secretly adored because she said things like that and because she was kind underneath her gruffness. I always felt safe—seen—in her classroom. And then there was another student of Chinese descent in my grade, but she was born in Savannah and had been going to school with the same people since kindergarten. She wasn't inclined to befriend me. The white expectation that she should and that perhaps we might somehow be related must have made it worse. I think my brother and I threatened the belonging that she had fought hard to earn.

My brother and I weren't keen on spending our Sunday afternoons with a bunch of old Chinese people we didn't know, either. The "clubhouse" was in a large, warehouse-like building in the middle of the woods with dirt roads into which our heels sank. The air-conditioning, a must in Savannah, barely worked and moaned so loudly that everyone inside always seemed to be shouting. The children were all much younger than we were. There was very little for us to do after politely greeting all the adults.

Then one day he walked in. His name was Rodney Jue. He was slim and tall and sometimes he showed up in his ROTC uniform. He was a senior at Benedictine, an all-boys military academy opened by Benedictine monks in Savannah in 1902. Even the way he walked, not with swagger but with ease, was unlike any Chinese person I've met in the U.S. up to that point. He had a white girlfriend named Karen who was petite, pale-skinned with dark hair, and had an air of boredom that told us she was only there *for him.* When he and his posse, including his cousin Robert and Robert's also-white girlfriend, arrived, the very vibration in the room changed. It was as if a noisy, aimless meeting suddenly morphed into a party with intention. Rodney and Robert liked to put on music and dance. I think it was the first time I had ever seen real people dance that way—everything from the Lindy Hop to hip-hop—right in front of me. When I watched them, it felt as if my feet were on fire inside my shoes, so eager was I to jump in, if I only knew how.

This group hardly ever seemed to notice the other people in the room. They came; they danced; they left. I don't think I ever spoke a single word to any of them, except Rodney, who made a point of introducing himself to me. He walked right up to me and asked who I was, after which he would always leave his group to spend a little time talking to me. He asked me about my school, my friends, and what I liked to do outside of school. I could see his bemusement when I said I liked to write poetry. I could also see his cohorts' curiosity laced with impatience. The few years between us felt like a huge gap. I was so far from his social world. Rodney looked at me with a mixture of interest, amusement, and mockery. His gaze made me feel pretty . . . and like an FOB.

My first crush: I was discovering myself in a room full of "my people" who weren't my kin, a sea of unfamiliar familiarity.

—

If/when the general American public thinks about the Chinese in America, they most likely think of the history of the "coolies" during the gold rush on the West Coast in the 1800s. Few think or know about Chinese sailors from what was called the China Trade, the early burgeoning commerce between the Qing Empire and the British Empire and colonial America. (The Boston Tea Party was precisely a fight over profits from this trade.) Some of those early Chinese sailors settled in New York City. Most of them lived in the immigrant quarters of Lower Manhattan and intermarried with immigrant Irish women, adopting their wives' surnames or otherwise Anglicizing their names, possibly to minimize discrimination against them or to reflect their conversion to Christianity. Thus one might find a John O'Leary or a William Longford in an early New York City census without realizing that these gentlemen were in fact "Chinamen."

And certainly almost no one thinks or knows about the history of the Chinese in the Deep South. Savannah was itself a burgeoning port that had dealt with direct trade with China since colonial times, since the *Empress of China* first sailed from America to China. Well-to-do Georgians were eager for Chinese goods like tea, silk, and porcelain. Religious Georgians, too, were greatly interested in spreading Christianity and missionary works in China. All through the eighteenth and nineteenth centuries, Georgian churches would host Chinese visitors to study Christianity with them. Finally, in the South, as in other places in the U.S., Chinese workers were recruited to fill the labor vacuum after the abolishment of slavery. They came to pick cotton in place of former slaves or to build infrastructure, including broadening the Augusta Canal. They were touted as "free, contract labor," though in reality their wages were so low and so siphoned off by discriminatory taxes and passage debts that those workers almost always found themselves forced to re-contract, effectively binding them to ongoing servitude. Stories swirled about them: they ate dogs and rats; their yellow skins made them impervious to sun and pain. The British philosopher Bertrand Russell noted that the Chinese had a natural proclivity for pain. He wrote in his 1922 treatise *The Problem of China* that Chinese men were known for their "passive endurance," that they "will endure torture, and even death, for motives which men of more pugnacious races would find insufficient." (Isn't this idea that the Chinese could quietly endure physical pain and repetitive boredom still with us today, with the repeated association of the Chinese with mechanistic, repetitive, uncre-ative labor, and the robotic?) This notion of Chinese male stam-ina, however, was seen as an aspect of their passivity rather than strength: the Chinese could bear pain and boredom because they were unimaginative. All this, of course, made the Chinese "coolies" at once ideal and disposable labor.

The early Chinese in the American South, merchants and laborers alike, lived in the cracks of a segregated system designed for Blacks and whites; they were maligned by the whites, who found them subhuman, and resented by Blacks, who saw them as competition. They took jobs that white men were unwilling to do. They socialized within their small communities and only ventured out to places they knew were safe. They were cogni-zant of their precarious position in the Black and white schism. Even in the Mississippi Delta area, where a large community of Chinese immigrants had settled and intermarried with African Americans for several generations, the Chinese continued to suf-fer both racism and xenophobia. They survived on tenterhooks, mostly ignored, barely tolerated, but always on the edge of being victims of violence.

The 1790 Naturalization Act permitted only "free white persons" to become naturalized citizens, thus opening the doors to European immigrants but not others. Asians were not allowed to naturalize into U.S. citizenship until the McCarran-Walter Act in 1952, and even then white racial preferences in immigration remained until 1965. (That's only roughly ten-plus years before my family's arrival.) With the exceptions of scholars and the merchant class, many of the male Asian workers who hadn't intended to stay found themselves stranded, stuck between the bondage of the "coolie contract" and race-based Asian exclusion laws that lasted almost a century, between 1875 and 1965, creating a largely aging population known as "Bachelor Societies" in segregated areas like the Chinatowns in major cities.

In California, at the height of nineteenth-century anti-Asian sentiments, alien land laws reserved farmlands for white growers by preventing Asian immigrants, ineligible to become citizens, from owning or leasing land. No such laws existed in Georgia, because for the most part the Georgia legislature didn't see the small number of Asians among them as much of a threat; their racial animus was focused primarily on African Americans. But as late as the 1960s, there were stories of whites not wanting or refusing to rent or sell to people of Asian descent. And inter-marriages, of course, remained anathema. Many of the recorded cases of anti-Chinese violence in the South involved Chinese men who married white women.

Knowing all this now makes me ashamed of my snotty teenage sense of superiority when I walked into the Canton Restaurant. I might have bemoaned the quality of the food, but looking back I realize that this shortcoming was also likely the very reason for the restaurant's long survival from 1930 to 1993. It must have been full of challenges and risks to open a Chinese restaurant in the South in the 1930s. Ingredients were hard to come by. Early Chinese restaurants in the South had to import vegetables like bok choy from San Francisco at great cost or make do with American vegetables. It would have been difficult to find and keep Chinese chefs, not to mention the staff. Then there was the challenge of getting the locals to try and take to this very foreign palate. The original Canton menu served something called mo kwat gai, which was basically southern fried chicken on a bed of lettuce with brown gravy.

I remember with pangs Mrs. Wu's stories of how in the early years people thought nothing of coming to eat and then leaving without paying. Or how other customers would talk with mock Chinese accents right in front of her husband and her as though they were deaf, didn't understand English, or were plain invisible. And how Mr. and Mrs. Wu trained their servers, and themselves, to endure silently, because acting otherwise ran the danger of courting violence. Nor did I know then that Mrs. Wu was a fierce activist who helped so many Chinese immigrants coming to the American South that Senator Herman Talmadge, former governor of Georgia, called her his "Chinese ambassador."

It isn't wholly accurate to say we were without family or were the only Taiwanese people in Savannah in the 1970s. There was, in fact, my uncle Tom, my mother's second-oldest brother. My mother has three brothers, twelve to fourteen years her senior. They all graduated at the top of their classes from the prestigious Táidà (National Taiwan University), then left Taiwan for America the minute they could in the years between 1950 and 1952.

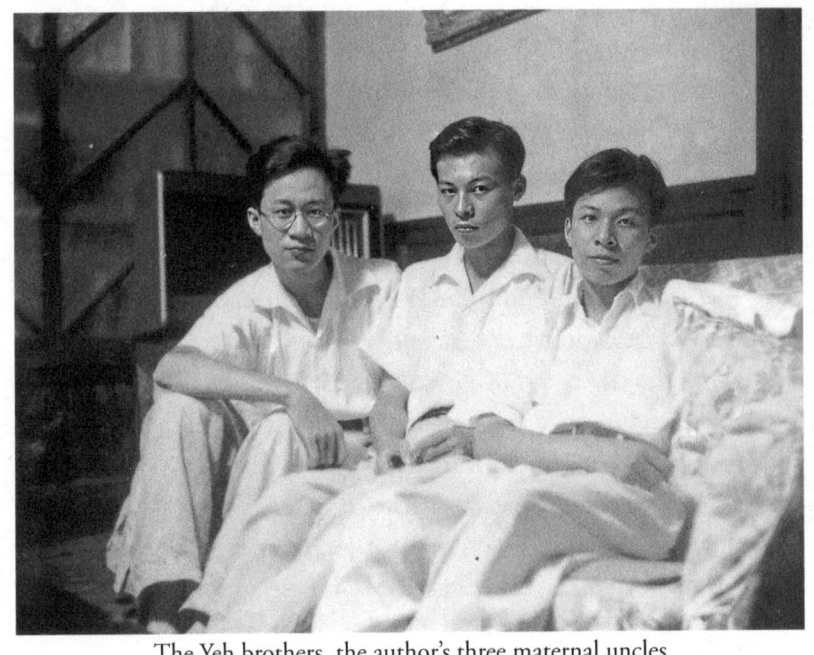

The Yeh brothers, the author's three maternal uncles

They couldn't wait to get out from under my grandfather's iron thumb and put an ocean between them. America represented freedom for them in many ways.

This did not stop my maternal grandfather from exerting his will on his sons or on his daughter and son-in-law. When thinking about moving to America, my father wanted to accept a position at Massachusetts General Hospital in Boston, but my mother, urged by her father, pushed for the Medical College of Georgia in Augusta, where her brother Tom, many years before, had worked as professor of surgery before settling down in Savannah. It makes sense, of course, when moving to a foreign country, that one would be pulled toward near relatives. But the truth was that my mother hardly knew her brother.

When Uncle Tom left Taiwan, my mother was still a child. By the time we arrived in Savannah, he had been established in Georgia for more than two decades. He was a well-known cardiothoracic surgeon who performed the first open-heart surgery in Savannah in the 1960s. He slept in his patient's room that first night because he couldn't be certain that the nurses were properly trained to deal with postsurgical care for what was back then a very new procedure. By the time we came, he was doing two, even three of these seven- to eight-hour surgeries a day. To me, he was a kind, soft-spoken man who dozed off the moment he sank into a sofa. He was married to my aunt Doris, a white woman from Kentucky who taught us how to bake pound cakes and make green bean casseroles. They married in the 1950s. Although my uncle and aunt never spoke to me about it, I wondered as an adult what discrimination they might have faced as a couple even if protected by, or in spite of, the shelter of his talents.

I had met my uncle only once before, in Taiwan, when he

came for a visit with his wife and two children. That was, as far as I knew, the only time he ever returned. I was about seven and didn't know yet that America was in my future. I recall that in my family the event was akin to the arrival of royalty. My grandparents came up to Taipei from Tainan to greet them. My mother fussed for weeks about how to feed and entertain them. My grandmother and my mom acted as self-appointed secretaries to manage the expectations of the extended family members who wanted at least a peek. Upon their arrival, I was fascinated by these relatives who seemed so foreign to me: my aunt's blond hair through which the sun shone; my cousins' brown hair streaked with gold; the way they talked. I was especially impressed by my cousin Karen, the prettiest girl I had ever seen, with her just as pretty dresses, and how brightly white her sneakers remained all the time. She even smelled different: clean, leafy, and what I would later identify as vanilla.

Although neither Karen nor her older brother, Tommy Jr., spoke Chinese, and neither my brother nor I knew English, we nonetheless got on famously, playing together all day and all evening until they left to go back to the hotel. We must have done a fair amount of air gesturing and signing, but I don't recall that. I remember only how much fun and laughter we had. Once, while we were all gathered in our living room, adults and kids alike, to enjoy bowls of cool almond gelatin, my brother inadvertently picked his nose in front of our special company, incurring horrified responses from my grandparents and parents, and he was promptly and emphatically told that *American children do not pick their noses.* As if on cue, just as my grandfather was giving my brother this valuable lesson, my cousin Tommy, oblivious to the conversation in Chinese, stuck his finger up his nose.

My cousins left behind cool gifts: pretty stickers; a tiny ball that bounced so high that you had to wait and watch for its return; a top that you wound up by rubbing its tip repeatedly on the ground before spinning it on top of an impossibly tiny red pedestal, smaller and lighter than a thimble. The top would spin madly around this center, generating its own centrifugal force. It was like watching a globe balancing on a pushpin. Back then, America seemed a strange world far away but one that could be easily mastered, like learning the ways of a new toy.

I don't know whether my mom actually recognized her brother when she saw him that time in Taiwan or whether that brief reunion made seeing him in America a few years later more natural. In America, we were the guests, even though we had our own house. My aunt and uncle were cordial and kind the way you were with in-laws, people whom you didn't know well but who suddenly became your close kin and moved next door. (We didn't move next door, but we did move several blocks down the same road, called Kent Drive.) In the beginning, my uncle switched between his faltering Taiwanese and his English, translating for my mom and to his wife. I, for one, was delighted to be reunited with my American cousins. Karen, kind as ever, quickly became my confidante and guide to all things American: trampoline, Uno, posters in the bedroom (not allowed in my house). Her older brother Tommy, now Thomas, was different. He didn't seem happy to see us this time. He often decamped to his room the minute we arrived. At times, he seemed downright angry at our very appearance. I was too young and self-involved to consider the preoccupations and turbulences of teenage boyhood, especially a biracial one in the South. I just felt terribly hurt that my cousin seemed ashamed of us, ashamed of either our immigrant uncouthness or the simple fact that we were Chinese.

What makes and unmakes a family, especially across time and migration? My uncle and his family were semi-strangers to us but our closest relatives in this new world. My uncle was Taiwanese, but not really anymore. We came from the same place, but our Americanness had different origins and came into being at a different pace. Behind my family's immigration were the invisible shadows of Taiwan's uncertain national destiny, the constant threat of mainland China, my parents' very real American Dream about our education, the vagaries of U.S. immigration and naturalization policies . . . and the will of an old man trying to control his children across the Pacific Ocean.

My grandfather thought that his son-in-law, my father, should follow his son's footsteps in America, even though my father had only met his brother-in-law once before coming to America, and my dad specialized in a different area of medicine. In truth, my grandfather's desire was simpler and more selfish: he liked the convenience of having his son and daughter in the same American city. (Looking back, I wondered how my dad, being a very proud and stubborn person himself, stomached his father-in-law's arrogant interventions through his and my mom's marriage.) For years, as long as I could remember and before we moved to the States, my grandparents would go and visit their three sons in America, in Hawaii, Los Angeles, and Georgia, their annual American tour. They never stayed more than a few days with each son. As far as I knew, my three uncles always accepted these visits and never failed to show their proper respect, but later as an adult I would come to see the cool formality with which my uncles treated their father. After we moved to the States, my grandparents started to extend their American tour from a week to six months at a time. They stayed with us, lived in our home, but my grandfather told friends and

Figure 1. Handmade dolls

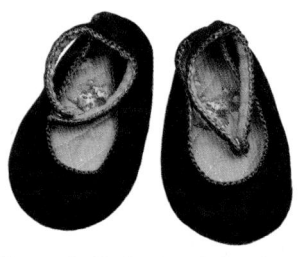

Figure 2. Red velvet baby shoes

Figure 3. Self-portrait as teenager, oil

Figure 4. Kim Novak, *Vertigo,*
dir. Alfred Hitchcock, 1958

Figure 5. Maggie Cheung, *In the Mood
for Love,* dir. Wong Kar-Wai, 2000
(Courtesy of Hulton Archive/Getty Images)

Figure 6. Diana Rigg,
The Avengers, 1961–69
(Courtesy of Shutterstock)

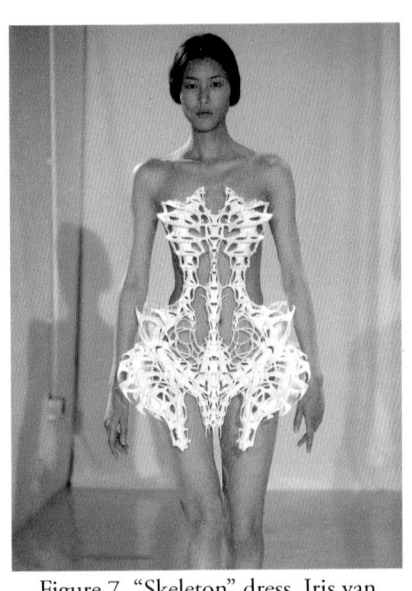

Figure 7. "Skeleton" dress, Iris van
Herpen, Haute Couture Fall 2011
*(Courtesy of Victor Virgile/Gamma-
Rapho/Getty Images)*

Figure 8. "Beijing Memory No. 5," Li Xiaofeng, 2009. Qing period shards. Red Gate Gallery, Beijing. Display from *China: Through the Looking Glass,* 2015, Metropolitan Museum of Art, New York.

Figure 9. *Harmless Kitty,* Yoshitomo Nara, 1994
(Courtesy of Yoshitomo Nara and Pace Gallery)

Figure 10. *Angry Little Asian Girl,* by Lela Lee
(Courtesy of Lela Lee)

Figure 11. *Blade Runner,* dir. Ridley Scott, 1982

Figure 12. *Ex Machina,* dir. Alex Garland, 2014

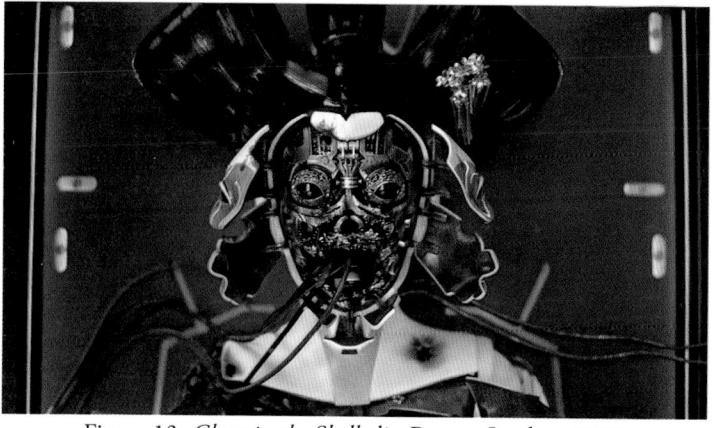

Figure 13. *Ghost in the Shell,* dir. Rupert Sanders, 2017

Figure 14. *Purple and Rose: The Lange Leizen of the Six Marks,*
James Abbott McNeill Whistler. Oil on canvas, 1864.
(Courtesy of the Philadelphia Museum of Art)

Figure 15. Display from *China: Through the Looking Glass,* Metropolitan
Museum of Art, 2015 *(Left)* Jar with dragon, Chinese, early fifteenth
century *(Right)* Evening dress, Roberto Cavalli, Fall/Winter 2005–2006

Figure 16. *Ex Machina*

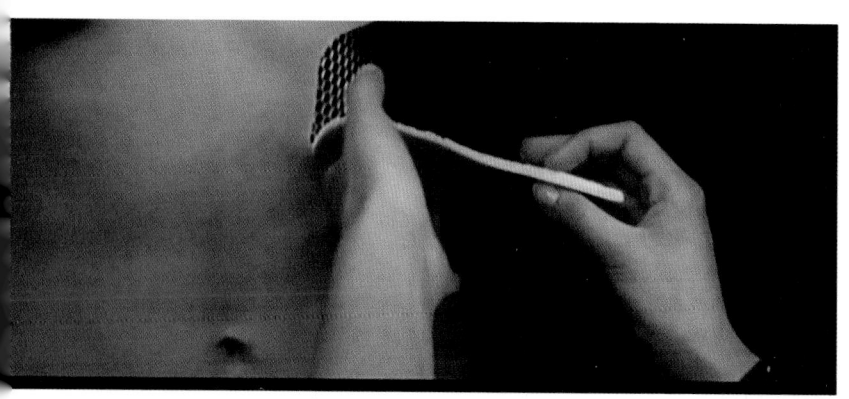

Figure 17. *Ex Machina*

Figure 18. The Canton, Savannah, Georgia
(Courtesy of the Wu family)

Figure 19. Chu's Department Store, Savannah, Georgia
(Courtesy of the Chu family)

relatives back in Taiwan that, in America, he lived with his son the heart surgeon. I remember when my mother first found out that he was telling this lie about where he lived. I could tell she was hurt, but she said she understood that her father would lose face if he had to admit that he had to stay at his daughter's rather than his son's.

When my grandfather died in Tainan, none of his sons showed up. That used to horrify me, and it took a while for me to realize that my grandfather, who was so indulgent with me, was also an unforgiving tyrant to his sons. It took time and age for me to understand that parents can love in different ways and that family ties, especially in a diaspora, always mean *something* even as they also always stand on the precipice of exposing their empty formality.

When my parents bought their first house in Savannah, Uncle Tom and Aunt Doris gave us a handsome dining room set that still sits in my mom's house. The huge, oval, oak table came with three extension leaves, even though at the time we didn't know enough people to populate it and my parents were still figuring their way through the maze of American sociality. My mother was moved by the generous gift but also anxious about appearing as poor relations who needed charity. She started cooking up a storm and bringing dinner to Uncle Tom's house almost every day. To her mind, he hadn't had decent Chinese food for over thirty years and surely must be craving it. And she was careful not to be intrusive; she would ring the bell and drop off the piping-hot dishes that she carefully timed for around dinnertime, just when she thought my uncle and his family would be sitting down to their meal. She couldn't understand why my aunt Doris, for all her good humor, appeared increasingly put out by the unsolicited delivery.

A year after we moved to Kent Drive, my uncle and aunt sold their house and moved to a newly built house by the water. And after my grandfather died and after all us kids graduated from high school and went away to college, the connection between us and Uncle Tom's household weakened. When my father died, my uncle didn't even call us. It's hard to write about this without sounding like I'm offering a reprimand. I really am not. The things that tied us together—our newness and neediness in America, my grandfather's willful expectations, our childhood friendships—are all things that passed. My mother and her brother went back to being relative strangers, this time in the same country, in the same city.

13

Unexceptional States

1.

A friend said the other day that all the places we used to think of as "Asian friendly"—San Francisco, Seattle, Los Angeles, New York, Vancouver—are now turning into hotspots of anti-Asian hatred and violence. Her comment depressed me not for its immediate truth but for its deeper insight about the Asian American and immigrant mindset even during unexceptional times. "Will we be safe there?" was the first question my mother asked some fifty-plus years ago when my parents first made the decision to immigrate to America.

Now people of Asian descent from all across the country are finding themselves being targeted, being yelled at or physically attacked: spat on, shoved, punched, kicked in the head, stabbed to death, pushed onto train tracks. The incidents I hear about on the news are happening to people I know, to dear friends. I walk down the street with anxious vigilance, and I worry about my elderly mother out in the world.

Being targeted for being Asian in America is not exceptional. It is the result and expression of more than three hundred years of cultural and legal discrimination directed first specifically against "the Chinese" in the 1800s and then, post–World War II, expanded more broadly against people from the "Asia Triangle" or the "Asiatic Barred Zone." African Americans have long understood that danger and denigration await them at every corner and haunt every exchange with strangers. And although Asians in America have been systematically characterized as an "exceptional" minority group—economically advantaged, seemingly overwhelming in numbers in certain sectors while perpetually foreign, which is also to say, hardly minor or American at all—their history in America, their very *American* history, is an erased-yet-integral part of the narrative of American Progress.

Recently, hard-right Republicans in the U.S. House of Representatives formed something called the America First Caucus, describing themselves as championing "Anglo-Saxon political traditions" and warning that mass immigration was putting the "unique identity" of the United States at risk. I wonder if individuals like Marjorie Taylor Greene and Matt Gaetz have studied their own racial-ethnic origins or know who the Anglo-Saxons really were and what their political traditions meant. This idea of a "pure America" that amounts essentially to a call for white supremacy and ethnic cleansing shows little understanding of the history behind the making of America. American historians have documented how the New World was polyglotted, transatlantic, and transpacific from the get-go, how an unprecedented expansion of trade and colonization in the early seventeenth century launched the first global economy, and how a vast, diverse, and landless workforce was born. The historians Peter Linebaugh and Marcus Rediker, for example, have documented how the roles of the dispossessed and the immigrant became foundational to the making of the modern world. According to their research, long before the American Revolution, the "Declaration of the Rights of Man," and the retroactive whitewashing of "American exceptionalism," a crew of sailors, slaves, pirates, laborers, market women, and indentured servants held and acted on ideas about freedom and equality that laid the foundation beneath the dreams of liberty and revolt. Workers who lit the fires of revolution were not only the Puritans but also those who crossed national, ethnic, and racial boundaries as they circulated around the Atlantic world on trade ships and slave ships, from England to Virginia, from Africa to Barbados, and from China to the Americas. America has always been—has never not been—a motley crew.

The "Big Lie" is not about the legitimacy of the 2020 presidential election. The real big lie is the belief in the racial purity of American origins and the myth of white supremacy that gave ideological cover to the long life of Western settler colonialism. That imagined history was created and has been preserved through violent, systemic erasures, aided by the painstaking *craft* of race-making (the legal and cultural processes through which certain immigrants became "white" and others became "Oriental") and its accompanying denials.

American history is populated by ghosts. Few people know that Chinese residents were the victims of one of the largest mass lynchings in America in Los Angeles's "Negro Alley" in 1871. Or that thousands of Chinese lives were sacrificed to the building of the Transcontinental Railroad, the backbone of American infrastructure and modern economy.

The famous photograph memorializing the celebration of the completion of the Transcontinental Railroad at Promontory Summit, Utah, in May 1869 was entitled "East Meets West" or "East and West Shake Hands." Scan the image: not a single Asian face can be found in this historic memory, even though

Photograph commemorating the completion of the first transcontinental railroad on May 10, 1869 *(Courtesy of the Beinecke Rare Book and Manuscript Library, Yale University)*

Chinese workers completed two-thirds of the most difficult stretches of the project and lost thousands of lives to it. The title of the photo refers, of course, to the railway connection of both coasts, making America the first nation to have unlimited access to both the Atlantic and Pacific Oceans, but the phrase "East Meets West" is also deeply ironic for those who know the critical yet erased roles that Chinese immigrant workers played in this American achievement.

Meanwhile, U.S. citizenship was busy consolidating itself through a series of legal racial exclusions (from the Chinese Exclusion Act to landmark cases like *Ozawa* and *Thind*), spelling out how the making of white American exceptionalism relied on the systematic erasure of an Other that it both needed and yet denied as integral to its formation. The price of this delicate and particularly American suspension—of keeping the racial Other close enough to be useful but not too close, incorporated but not assimilated, consumed but not digested—is what I have in my scholarship named "American racial melancholia": an unacknowledged loss incorporated as a ghostly, undigested presence in the belly of American polity. Systems of colonialism, internment, segregation—all of which America has availed itself of—operate not by fully expelling the racial Other but by securing without recognizing the Other within existing institutions. This is what makes the American racial ecology and American democracy so specific and volatile: an elaborate structure built on the diversity that it disavows.

Asian Americans have known, experienced, and worried about this antagonism for a long time. We have been habituated to its mild quotidian forms and anticipated its more explicit expressions. It takes very little for the scale to tip. Throughout the centuries we remain tethered to the specter of the yellow peril, which attaches itself to us again and again, from the violent efforts to "expel the Chinese" in the nineteenth century and the demonization of the Asian, both abroad and domestically, throughout the twentieth century: during times of national crisis (the American internment of Japanese Americans during World War II); in periods of economic downturn (the threat of Asian economic rise leading to the murder of Vincent Chin and the persecution of Wen Ho Lee in the 1980s, revived today as the harassment of Chinese American scientists in the academy); and, of course, during times of disease (the phrase *China virus* simply naming the conflation of Asia with contagion). The specter of yellow peril also undergirds the exoticization of Asian women ("yellow fever") as well as the faint praise behind the image of the model minority (hardworking but deeply unlikable and always quietly threatening).

Lately I've started to keep count compulsively: a global pandemic, especially deadly for the physically weak and the economically vulnerable; rapid climate changes that flooded half of the nation while engulfing the other half in flames; an insurgence at our nation's capital by a mob carrying the Confederate flag; the senseless killing of Black men and women on an almost daily basis; the shameless, murderous attacks on innocent Asian American elderly people, women, and children; a humanitarian crisis erupting at the borders; mass shooting becoming a regular occurrence . . . and, all the while and perhaps most egregious, a large part of the nation in willful denial of any of these catastrophes.

To deny what is happening all around us is to acknowledge that hatred and violence have become the tolerable conditions of our lives. America has spent decades disavowing its foundational paradox of freedom built on unfreedom—what the sociologist

Michael Rogin called the Janus-faced origins of the United States Constitution—and has now come to a bald-faced acceptance of violent hatred as its unexceptional condition.

I spent decades teaching my students what now seem lofty ideas about ethical responsibility; the limits of identity politics; the easy, fragile morality touted by the righteous on both sides of the political aisle; and democracy's profound complicity with colonialism and other racist institutions. But these days I feel like I need to step way back in the classroom and talk about the basics: civility, empathy, common good.

2.

I once heard a young man ask my friend the poet who writes about the beauty and grief of human wishes whether he, that is, the young man himself, ought to be suffering for his art. And my friend had replied, gently, "You do not have to worry about that. Life will take care of that for you."

When the phone call came that turned my world upside down on a blissfully quiet Saturday, I did not at first understand what was being said to me. The doctor never used the C-word; she spoke carefully of an unusually large tumor on my right ovary and how I needed to find a surgeon ASAP. She recommended somewhere called Fox Chase. I looked it up, and the full name reads, "Fox Chase Cancer Center."

Part of me was disbelieving. I have no family history of cancer, and hadn't I always done the right things, exercised, and eaten clean?

Part of me thought, well, there it is, my malignant body.

I have always been, at least as an adult, someone who is constantly on the lookout for the unforeseen, the things that could go wrong. This preparedness is what made me the go-to person for problem solving at work and a good mother of small children. This is also what made me unbearable to loved ones who have had to suffer my worst-case scenarios. It is really a kind of superstition, the idea (in truth, the talismanic hope) that if you anticipate it enough, the bad won't come your way, just as if you carry an umbrella, it won't rain.

It is hard to accept that good and bad things happen to people, regardless of whether they anticipate or deserve it. It's hard to accept because it means that we have no control over the vagaries of fortune. And for a Taiwanese immigrant who grew up in the American South, if I don't have *striving*—and the promised results of that concerted labor—then what do I have?

Cancer and chemo turned out to be lessons in letting go. The moment I got the diagnosis, my life and body became questions already answered, given over to the medical machinery. I went from a purposeful person responding to the thousands of little decisions and demands of motherhood and professional and daily life to following protocols so honed and so universal that the doctor opened up a chart to show me where I fell on it and the combination of specific chemicals required to save and erase me.

There was almost a relief in such clarity.

I could be content on a quiet weekend morning, rehearsing my list of things to do while my family slept peacefully around me, when a call out of the blue changed everything. I could be walking down the street, absorbed in random thoughts, when two young men, the age of my students, strolled past on either side of me, suddenly body-slammed into me, their hands grabbing my jacket and yanking it hard off my shoulders, then walked on casually. (If such malice would hardly be called real violence, then why was my heart pounding in my chest?)

It always takes a minute or two to register, to transition from the me that is *me* to the me that is an object in the world.

I am prey to many ugly feelings, but what I hate most is fear. I dread that heated tightening radiating through my veins, filling up my stomach and chest, a repeated explosion without relief. Fear that I will have to say good-bye to loved ones sooner than expected. Fear that I may have to lose more body parts, or that I will have to go through chemo again. Fear that even as my immune functions start to recover, I now have to worry about taking the subway alone in Manhattan. Fear that I can wrap myself up in American civility and education, and yet I will always remain raw and naked.

3.

Upon hearing about my diagnosis, a friend who's a physician recommended that I not google ovarian cancer. I, of course, already had. And he was right to warn me away. "Ovarian cancer is the most deadly gynecologic cancer, with approximately 45% of patients surviving only 5 years. The death rate from ovarian cancer has changed very little in the past 40 years."

In two years, my daughter will graduate from college and my son will be in college. I have to adjust my ambitions. I used to dream about seeing my kids with their own children. Now I hope I get to attend my daughter's graduation. It would be something to make it to my son's.

There are people I know and care about who are living with the knowledge of their certain death, and they are navigating this wait with more grace than I can imagine. But I am stuck in a gamble. I pinball between calculations: the CA-125 (cancer antigen marker), the 50/50 chance that might have been improved by surgery to 70/30, or by chemo to 80/20, depending on who's giving the information. My life turns on a number. I don't know whether it is better to live with the full reminder that I could die in the next few years or to move forward the way normal people do, not thinking they will live forever but without a sense of limit. Which will allow me to have the most faith in the moment and its endurance?

I keep returning to that moment in Olaudah Equiano's memoir when he wrote that he thought the clock and the portrait in the white man's house were watching him and about to tell on him. (And, of course, in a sense, they were, being symbols of surveillance and control.) Or of Ralph Ellison's invisible man who, on an accidental street collision, beat the white man down before the latter could strike. A messy web of sight and insight: one could accuse the invisible man of paranoia, and he might have been, but at the same time he would have been blind or stupid not to suspect that a racist confrontation was about to ensue.

Cancer and racism: diseases at the most cellular level, killing the biological body and the body politic. Both render the distinction between paranoia and perspicacity impossible. There are scripts that we follow, and scripts that follow us.

14

Affirmative Action

Years ago, when I was a newly tenured faculty, in a departmental discussion on the pros and cons of affirmative action, a much more senior colleague stood up and pointed (literally) to me as a good example of affirmative action. At the time, I was horrified by the sudden attention of forty-plus pairs of eyes on me. My first thought was that Asian Americans were not considered underrepresented minorities in the UC system or on the West Coast. My second thought was that my work is so much more than that! But deep inside I felt affronted by what had seemed to me then the suggestion that somehow I got my position through less than hard work or for less than intellectual reasons.

In a society that values self-determination, nothing is more vexing—or more misunderstood—than affirmative action. Most individuals of color do not want to be told that they owe their jobs or their recognition to affirmative action, while disgruntled whites begrudge the opportunities that they imagined have been denied to them due to it.

Although there are plenty of negative feelings swirling around the issue, there are plenty of confusions, too. Who counts as underrepresented? In what fields and under what contexts? Who actually is most likely to benefit from the elimination of affirmative action?

The drama of affirmative action being played out in the public eye often looks like something out of *The Hunger Games* among communities of color. The 2023 Supreme Court cases over college admission, for instance, frame the issue as a rivalry between Asian Americans and African Americans. The plaintiffs, a small group of Asian Americans who call themselves Students for Fair Admissions, argued to the high court that Harvard College discriminates against Asian American applicants because, under affirmative action, they are less likely to be admitted than Black and Hispanic applicants with similar qualifications. The group has also sued the University of North Carolina, a public university, over its use of race in college admissions.

These lawsuits tap into a series of long-standing assumptions and anxieties: (1) that affirmative action is inherently anti-merit; (2) that it is the "nerdy Asians" who are the most threatened by this policy; and (3) that affirmative action only benefits African Americans.

Reality and common sense tell us otherwise. First and most explicitly, *no one* gets into college based on race alone, even with affirmative action in play. Race—along with class, gender, geography, and extracurricular and academic interests—constitutes but one factor in an elaborate and complex equation that we call college admission. Second, research has documented how effective affirmative action has been in increasing racial diversity. (In the real-life case of the University of California system: after Proposition 209 eliminated affirmative action, the number of Black students dropped precipitously.) Third, when it comes to Asian Americans, most experts agree that the end of affirmative action will *not* change discrimination against Asian Americans.

There is no such a thing as "pure merit," and even if there were, Asian Americans would not necessarily benefit from such standards. In college admission, the elusive calculus of "merit" falls into two different forms of assessment: so-called hard versus soft ranking. The former encompasses quantifiable grades and test scores; the latter refers to ineffable qualities such as creativity, maturity, and social skills. Since Asian Americans are stereotypically seen as uncreative, immature, and socially inept, they tend to score low in the "soft merit" category. At the same time, should Asian American candidates exhibit stellar "hard" numbers, they are often dismissed as one-dimensional grinds. Asian American candidates are thus the only racial group that can simultaneously be seen as too good and not good enough. Finally, recent surveys, conducted by AAPI Data and PEW between 2020 and 2022, show that 69 to 70 percent of Asian Americans continue to approve of and support affirmative action. The group Students for Fair Admissions therefore does not represent the Asian American community at large.

So how is it that an ongoing conservative white anxiety about Black integration, couched as a concern about the decline of American meritocracy, should be played out as a bitter competition between Asian Americans and African Americans? The long and broader answer is the chimera of American racial triangulation. The short answer is Edward Blum.

Blum is a white, conservative legal strategist who has been working toward the end of race-based admissions in higher education for years. He was the force behind *Shelby County v. Holder,* the 2013 Supreme Court ruling that rolled back voting rights, making it harder for ethnic minorities to vote. Since then he has turned his focus on eliminating the use of race and ethnicity in college admissions. He had initially cast two white women, most notably Abigail Fisher, to craft lawsuits intended to end affirmative action, claiming that affirmative action was racist against white people. When both cases lost, Blum had to pivot in his strategy. He went to a Chinese American association in Houston, Texas, and persuaded a dozen or so Chinese Americans in the conference room that their children's college futures were being jeopardized by affirmative action. Blum was not even that subtle about it; as he told his audience, "I needed new plaintiffs . . . I needed *Asian* plaintiffs."

In short, what happened with the 2022 Supreme Court cases is not a natural outcome of Asian American and African American competition. Asian Americans—here, the Students for Fair Admissions—are being used as stand-ins for white, anti-Black interests, just as the "model minority" had historically been deployed as a proxy for white conservatives to shame other racialized minorities and to critique the welfare system. Asian Americans end up being props for the fantasy of colorblindness, tools in a cynical scheme to deflect away from the reality that anything might be "taken away" from whites.

Strategists like Blum and his orchestrated legal campaigns stoke Asian immigrant, parental anxieties about how their children are being discriminated against and how other racialized minorities are reaping benefits at their expense. Asian Americans, of course, do suffer discrimination, except the source of that discrimination is being misdirected. Anti-Asian discrimination is less likely to come from affirmative action policies than from the host of stereotypes that haunt Asian American candidates, especially the image of Asian Americans as drone-like overachievers.

But the biggest misunderstanding and the most egregious boondoggle in the 2022 Supreme Court decision is how the pre-

dominantly conservative Court cited, as its rationale, the landmark 1954 case of *Brown v. Board of Education* as precedent for
the doctrine of "Constitutional colorblindness." To paraphrase
the high court's logic, since the Constitution is "colorblind," it
is therefore unconstitutional to take race into consideration.
This reasoning would have us believe that a decades-long solution aimed to foster racial diversity in the face of systemic and
historic racial inequality is itself racist because it recognizes race.
What convoluted and perverse logic!

What's sad is that the history of *Brown* is itself beset by this
kind of pernicious logic. We tend to think of *Brown* as this water-
shed moment when American apartheid gave way, but *Brown*
and its legacy is much messier than that. It took more than ten
years after *Brown* for the American school system to become
fully desegregated. In 1963, almost a decade after *Brown,* in my
hometown of Savannah, Georgia, a lawsuit (*Stell v. Savannah-
Chatham County Board of Education*) was filed by a group of
African American parents against the Chatham County board
for conducting what was called at the time "biracial" education;
that is, the county had integrated African American and white
children in the schools but not in the classrooms, thus a de facto
segregation was still in place. In that case, a group of white,
pro-segregation parents joined the defense and, in a surprising
move, cited the same Clark study used by Marshall to argue for
segregation, contending that since Black students suffered from
the lack of self-esteem, a "separate education" would grant Black
children the opportunity to develop a stronger, "healthier" Black
identity "among their own." Thus the very evidence that Marshall drew on to prove racial injury caused by segregation was
being used to support the isolation and continued segregation
of Black students. A discourse of *identity affirmation,* supposedly

for independent Black identity, turned into a weapon for white supremacy.

To take Marshall's argument against the use of race as a basis for discrimination (i.e., that it is unconstitutional to segregate by race) and turn it into an argument for not seeing race ("colorblindness") in a policy meant to address inequality, as the majority of the justices on the Supreme Court recently did, is more than revisionist; it is downright reprehensible. Clarence Thomas, in particular, should be ashamed—not because all African Americans should support affirmative action, nor even because he is from Savannah and should be aware of the history behind the hard-earned progress of American civil rights, but rather because he has himself experienced discriminatory hiring practices. In his autobiography, Thomas wrote about how, as a promising graduate from Yale Law School in the 1970s, he had really wanted to be a corporate lawyer, but corporate jobs for Black lawyers were hard to come by, and he was forced instead to go into government work. That government work, in a twist of irony, would take him to the highest court in the land, where he proceeded to vote against affirmative action. (Let's remember, too, that women had a hard time finding employment in the legal profession. Ruth Bader Ginsburg graduated first in her class from Columbia Law School but could not find a job and had to go into teaching. All this makes Thomas's treatment and defamation of a woman, his colleague Anita Hill, for the price of his seat on the Court, all the more indefensible.)

Thomas's decades-long push for "colorblindness" reeks of disavowal and reaction formation. He compensated for and erased the racial denigration he himself experienced by replacing it with a narrative of his own bootstrap, individualist talent, a narrative of personal achievement that is in turn jeopardized by the specter of a public policy that might have suggested his success was anything but personal aptitude. Thus even as white conservatives use colorblindness as a front for thwarting Black interests, Black conservatives like Thomas play right into that strategy. The former are trying to preserve their privilege; the latter are trying to preserve their ego.

Let us be clear: colorblindness *only* works in a nonracist world, and we *know* we do not live in such a world.

In a racist society, worse than mere neutrality, colorblindness becomes an alibi for actively maintaining inequality. What the constitutional scholar Neil Gotanda wrote several decades ago still holds: "A colorblind interpretation of the Constitution legitimates, and thereby maintains, the social, economic, and political advantages that whites hold over other Americans." In the same study, Gotanda traced how the modern legal use of "colorblindness" emerged *after* the passage of the Thirteenth, Fourteenth, and Fifteenth Amendments and after *Brown*. In other words, the discourse of colorblindness arose as a reactionary response to the development of civil rights. (Similarly, most of the Civil War memorials across the American South were initially erected not after the Civil War, as one would suspect, but years later during the civil rights era.) And as Justice Sonia Sotomayor articulated in her dissenting opinion: "The Court cements a superficial rule of colorblindness as a constitutional principle in an endemically segregated society where race has always mattered and continues to matter . . . Equality requires acknowledgement of inequality."

Separate is inherently unequal.

In a racially riven world, *colorblindness, too, is inherently unequal.*

Over the years I have pondered my own unspoken allergy to

the idea of affirmative action. Nor have I ever liked being called "the first!" or designated as "the role model." It's never comfortable to be reduced to one's symbolic value. But now I think it is no small thing to be shown possibilities one has not imagined before or to be given a chance where none had existed before. Looking back to that faculty meeting so many years ago, I see that my unease in that room spoke more to my own insecurities than anything else. No one is more prone to the imposter syndrome than an academic, especially an academic woman of color. My unease also said something about my own convoluted path. How did a Taiwanese girl who came to America refusing to learn the alphabet until the last desperate moment become an English professor?

In college, to my parents' horror, I majored in English literature, specializing in British modernism. (Years later, at some reunion, a classmate I didn't remember recognized me by saying, "Oh, you were *that* Chinese girl who majored in English!") While I genuinely loved—and still love—the writers I studied, I was not unaware of how my intellectual choices were bucking against expectations. No, I wasn't going to be a mathematician or engineer or doctor. No, I wasn't an East Asian studies major. I wasn't going to "study myself," which seemed self-involved and intellectually suspicious.

But why did I think that? White students don't feel solipsistic or intellectually illegitimate when they study Shakespeare or James Joyce or when they major in American studies. I was in fact shaped by the clichés I thought I was eschewing. In not giving in to stereotypes, I ended up denying large parts of myself. What I didn't realize as a young person was that when I shied away from East Asian studies, or American studies, for that matter, I also foreclosed from myself fields of knowledge and communities that might have spoken to my young self's private, ongoing struggles with what it means to be American, Asian, and Asian American.

I didn't discover Asian American studies as a field until I was in graduate school doing something else. And even then the field filled me with as much frustration as elation. It had seemed to me then that the identity politics of the 1980s and '90s ended up reproducing identity silos and ideologies of cultural authenticity that felt highly problematic to me. Identity, after all, *is* the same ground on which both affirmation and discrimination are made. This is how racial affirmation and racist rejection share the same language. But over the years I also came to see how difficult and dangerous it can be to question identity for those who never enjoyed recognition in the first place or for those who never acknowledged how certain identities have been, materially and legally, placed at risk or under erasure.

Affirmative action is fraught not only because of the persistent question about merit but also because of the flattening out of an individual to a racial category. This is endemic to most of our current institutional efforts to "correct" racism: a flat-footed quantitative numbers game or an ineffectual moralism aimed at addressing a complex, systematic, widespread, and discriminatory system that breeds both quantifiable and hard-to-quantify consequences. But having limited tools does not mean we stop using them, refining them. Progress is slow and its rollback heartbreakingly easy. It took decades to desegregate our nation. Many will point out that we are still fighting this battle. In the past several years alone, so much hard-earned progress has been decimated: women's rights, civil rights, environmental protection. (The Environmental Protection Agency was practically dismantled during the Trump presidency.)

Yes, affirmative action is vexing for persons of color. So, too, is identity: at once vital and limiting. I flinch when white readers expect writers of Asian descent to write about "being Asian." Equally, I wince when I hear writers of Asian descent insist that they are American, rather than Asian American, writers. I understand that a writer of color might not want to be pigeonholed, or be reduced to an ethnographic/cultural guide, or be seen as performing or trading in on their ethnicity. At the same time, why do we assume that to be an "Asian American writer" is restrictive instead of being generative and creative? As the scholar Min Hyoung Song elegantly put it, "Is your individuality so important that you refuse to be tainted by the possibility that you are part of something larger, collectivities that bind and narrow . . . as much as they enable and support and make impossible things seem suddenly, breathtakingly possible after all?"

Affirmative action remains an imperfect but still necessary answer to a very broken system.

When I look at my students, each striving to prove their worth and virtuosity, I think of Malcolm Gladwell's insight in *Outlier* that success does not come solely or even primarily from IQ or innate talent but rather from the ability to recognize a given opportunity and to make the most of it. The key here is the *given:* not the kind of given that is unquestioned and already in place, like privilege, but given as in something that someone or some mechanism extended and made available that would otherwise not have been. Success, which to me means building a life that is meaningful and sustaining, a difficult enough task, requires a great deal of hard, ongoing, personal labor, but it also takes luck and community. I think of all the people who have given me a chance *for whatever reasons*—the college interviewer who spoke to a green Taiwanese teenager in Savannah, Georgia; the teacher who said, "You should think seriously about writing"; the adviser who stepped in to rephrase a hostile question during my PhD oral exam—and I am deeply grateful for all the opened windows.

15

Then, Atlanta

Going to high school in Savannah, Georgia, I was pretty much the perpetual alien. I wrote poetry while others tailgated. I lost myself in James Joyce and Virginia Woolf while my peers went to debutante balls. (The whole "coming out" business, with its showy, genteel announcement that the Girl Is Now Open for Business, mystified me. What would happen if a girl ever decided to remain "in"?) I went to school dressed in black while my cohorts sported alligators and whales in pink and green. I was driving my mom's lime-green Pontiac, the one on sale in the lot, while others were zooming by in their Porsches and Ferraris. And, of course, I was Chinese and not southern.

Although I would come to love Savannah, I hated it when we first moved there. I was just getting used to the red, hilly earth of Augusta, and then we moved to the swamps. As a child I found the ubiquitous Spanish moss spooky (I imagined it to be some parasitic strangler of trees), the dilapidated old mansions downtown depressing, and the marshlands, especially during low tide, dank and murky.

I loved it when my family escaped to go to Atlanta, which became, surprisingly, our Asian retreat. In the 1970s, Atlanta had a Japanese grocery and a handful of decent Japanese and Chinese restaurants. There was even a Chinese bookstore. My family would drive the six hours to Atlanta whenever my dad was not on call on a weekend or when my mom could no longer make do with the local Piggly Wiggly.

No one thinks of a southern city as a multiracial heaven, but as early as 1913 a local reporter had referred to Decatur Street, the main drag of downtown Atlanta's working-class, mixed-race residential and commercial district, as "the melting pot of Dixie," although the reporter was talking mostly about European immigrants and Jews rather than Asians. But after the liberalization of American immigration policy in 1965 (with the Hart-Celler Act), people from Asia, Africa, the Caribbean, and Latin America began to settle throughout the South. By the time the 1996 Olympics came to town, Atlanta was known as a "gateway city" for a new wave of immigration to the United States.

Today, the metro Atlanta region, which includes nearly two dozen counties surrounding the urban core, is home to the second-fastest-growing foreign-born population in the United States. Though stigmatized and marginalized by laws and regulations directed at undocumented aliens, these new groups have developed their own bustling neighborhoods in the outermost edges of the city, and in some locations have come to constitute a sizable population in metro-area towns and school districts. Atlanta's Buford Highway, where my family used to visit regularly, has since become one of the most intensely concentrated ethnic-owned business corridors in the Southeast, known for its Chinese, Vietnamese, Hmong, Korean, and Mexican restaurants and groceries. All along Buford Highway in Gwinnett County, where we used to find the one good sushi restaurant, now boasts of everything from dim sum to sashimi to pho to dosa. The small market that my family used to visit has expanded into a huge shopping area with an internationally renowned farmer's market. Today more than sixty-three thousand people in Gwinnett County speak an Asian language at home.

My father, who is no longer with us and who used to love exploring Atlanta, would be astounded and delighted by what we can now find there. I can see him, if he were with us now, testing out the different sushi restaurants and ranking them before deciding to which he will devote his allegiance. I can see him and my mom spending whole weekends there instead of the quick one-day jaunts they used to do. I can see myself flying in alone and meeting them there, reliving and retreating into familial habits, old immaturities, cradled by the unexpected familiarity of our very own Asian Atlanta.

Then, *that* Atlanta happened.

On March 16, 2021, a twenty-one-year-old white man drove first to Cherokee and then to Fulton County, neighborhoods northeast of downtown Atlanta, commonly known to be "culturally diverse." There he targeted three Asian-owned spas and went on a shooting spree, killing eight people, six of them women of Asian descent. This came on the heels of a precipitous rise in anti-Asian violence nationwide, mostly perpetrated against Asian and Asian American women and elderly.

When the incident happened, the Atlanta police were reluctant to call it a hate crime motivated by racism. Why not? Because the shooter told the authorities that he suffered from a "sex addiction." The police chief stated in a press conference that the young man "was having a bad day." FBI Director Chris Wray said, according to his initial assessment, that race "does not appear" to have played a role in the shooting. And almost immediately after the news broke late that Wednesday night, a certain kind of response started popping up on Twitter: "No happy ending then?" " 'Youngs Asian' massage parlour . . . they love you long time." Social media comments are notorious for their allergy to thoughtfulness, but these brutal jokes speak to a prejudice that is deeply ingrained, if largely unacknowledged, in American society. The shootings took place within an escalating pattern of anti-Asian violence, but they also speak directly to a long history of the simultaneous erotization and denigration of Asian women that is as old as the birth of Western imperial ambition itself. They cast light on the continual association and criminalization of Asian women with sex work and the American male fantasies of entitlement to Asian female bodies.

For many women of color, the idea that misogyny and racism can go hand in hand is a fact of life. Almost every woman of Asian descent I know who grew up in America has experienced some version of strange men's unctuous hailing or intrusive come-ons that mix flattery with a vague sense of threat. As a young woman on the receiving end of such unwanted attention, I never said anything about it, because I understood that most people would consider such incidents minor inconveniences, even though the encounters always produced a sickening sensation in the pit of my stomach.

When Atlanta happened, that sickening sensation grew into a pain. Watching law enforcement relay the shooter's explanation was an exercise in both disbelief and recognition. It was a harsh reminder that these acts were a very real, very lethal manifestation of what goes unspoken behind all those seemingly harmless, supposedly flattering solicitations that dog Asian women: a profound disregard for them as people, an aggressive imputation of their imagined availability, and a deep assumption of racial and masculine prerogative. As a woman of middle-class privilege, I have been mostly sheltered from the harsher forms of this aggression, but it is a grave mistake not to understand that "mild" and "violent" racist sexism thrive on the same continuum. Here's the thing that many people find hard to accept: *Hatred does not preclude desire. Hatred legitimizes the violent expression of desire.*

By his own admission, the shooter could not control *his* desires, so he went out to eradicate the objects of his desires. Is there a more stark articulation of the projective force and killing intent of racist misogyny?

Racism and sexism are partners that stoke each other with frightening ease. Racism may be caused by many factors—demagoguery, religious intolerance, economic resentment, inherited bigotry—but its expression is almost always about the assertion of power. And whenever revengeful male power is in play, it is never good news for women.

Anti-Asian racism and long-standing Western colonial attitudes about the plunderable "Orient" enable the possessive denigration and dehumanization of Asian women; patriarchy and sexism further fortify such presumptions. The figure of the eroticized-yet-degraded Asian woman—also known as "China doll," "lotus blossom," "geisha," "concubine," and "butterfly"—can be readily found in movies and onstage, in everything from high art to cheap pornography.

Historically and even legally, America has long conflated Asian female sexuality with criminality. The first time Chinese litigants appeared before the U.S. Supreme Court was in 1875, in *Chy Lung v. Freeman,* which involved the perception and legislation of Chinese women as prostitutes. Sensationally known in contemporary papers then as the "Case of the 22 Lewd Chinese Women," the case centered on a group of young women who were denied entry into the U.S. at the Port of San Francisco despite having proper travel documentation (and despite the Burlingame Treaty, which allowed for such migration), as the local state immigration inspector thought they *looked like* prostitutes because they were traveling alone. The trial transcript revealed a dog and pony show where the serious legal issue of state-versus-federal authority over immigration turned on inquiries such as what the women were or were not wearing: the colors of their underskirts or a brocade collar, the style of head kerchiefs, the width of a sleeve. (This was apparently how you could tell a respectful Chinese housewife from a prostitute.) The state of California argued that it had the right to protect itself from the "pestilential immorality" represented by these young Chinese women. The Supreme Court eventually ruled in favor of the women, not because they thought the women were innocent but because they wanted to affirm the federal government's authority over the States to regulate immigration rights.

It was partially in backlash to this supposed "Chinese victory" that in the same year the United States passed the Page Act, introduced by Representative Horace Page of California, to "end the danger of cheap Chinese labor and immoral Chinese women." Apparently, to California officials, all Chinese women were prostitutes. The Page Act was the first restrictive federal immigration law in the U.S., effectively prohibiting the entry of Chinese women into the country. It foreshadowed the more stringent Chinese Exclusion Act to follow, which in turn produced the mostly male "Bachelor Societies" of American Chinatowns, placing the few Asian women who were here in even more physical, social, and economic jeopardy. In the twentieth century, U.S. foreign policy sent American soldiers abroad to

Asia, introducing to the racial-sexual imagination about Asian women new variations of a familiar figure, creating a malevolent lineage of "prostitute" to "comfort women" to the "war bride" to the "sex worker."

That the murdered women in Atlanta worked in massage parlors—spaces that are deeply racialized and sexualized in the American and global consciousness—only underscores the continued invisibility and precarity of immigrants and service-industry workers.

Let me name the victims: Delaina Ashley Yaun, 33; Xiaojie Tan, 49; Daoyou Feng, 44; Paul Andre Michels, 54; Hyun Jung Grant, 51; Soon Chung Park, 74; Suncha Kim, 69; Yong Ae Yue, 63. Xiaojie Tan was days away from her fiftieth birthday and is survived by her husband and a daughter who recently graduated from college. Yong Ae Yue was a working mother, as was Hyun Jung, a single mother working overtime to raise two sons.

These women were workers, mothers, wives—persons who, we must insist again and again, lost their lives to one individual's desires and to a larger culture of racialized misogyny.

16

Asian Pessimism

In the past three years, there have been five student suicides on my home campus. All five students were Asian American. Institutional powers did not underscore this fact. Few, in fact, seemed to notice. But my Asian American students noticed.

Public conversations about Asian American mental health are almost nonexistent. This neglect is often attributed to "Asian culture" itself, that is, Asian cultures stigmatize mental illness, and so Asian Americans often fail to seek mental health assistance due to shame and embarrassment. They are inclined to suck it up and agonize in silence. In short, the model minority. Given what is happening out in the world to Asian Americans, is it that they don't speak up or that they are not heard? And if the narrative of the stoic model minority were true, should it not compel us all the more to question the outcome and cost of being such a figure?

My students want to know why no one is talking about what is happening to their peers. I look into their eyes and see a mixture of anxiety, uncertainty, anger, sorrow, and sometimes something akin to recognition. None of us can speak to the specificities of these tragedies. Our minds scramble and fail to grasp such unmitigated loss and what it says about the private depths of hopelessness. But I know we need to start a sustained, not just reactive, conversation about Asian American emotional health. How does violence on the outside get lived as violence on the inside? How are Asian American aspiration and success tied to, rather than serve as antidotes for, Asian American grief?

There are those who imagine university campuses to be safe, natural habitats for the studious Asian. These are likely some of the same people who fret about how Asians are overrunning American universities. But according to the National Center for Educational Statistics, with the exceptions of the Ivy League and a handful of elite institutions, the percentage of Asian Americans in most degree-granting postsecondary institutions in the U.S. are, in fact, quite low, much lower than other minority groups, such as African American and Hispanic students. And in the cases of those elite institutions, the conversation should be less about enrollment numbers and more about how Asian Americans are treated.

The sources of denigration within those sacred academic walls can be both mundane and devastating. In December 2022, at Purdue University's graduation ceremony, the university chancellor got up onstage and made a series of cacophonous, "ching-chong" noises that clearly intended to imitate Chinese speech, as a joke. Worse yet, almost as soon as this story reached the news, the conversation shifted from the meaning of the incident for Asian Americans to a fixation on the unfortunate chancellor's career and whether or not he had been a victim of so-called cancel culture. To wit, *The New York Times* published an op-ed called "When a Racist Joke Does Not Merit Cancellation," by John McWhorter, which bemoaned our nation's current tendency these days toward "devolving into the Jacobinesque routines of cancel culture." In the article, McWhorter, who is African American, conceded that the chancellor's performance was in bad taste but also asked, "How *much* racism is in question here?" In other words, are Asian Americans injured, or injured enough, to deserve our attention?

No one asked: What is this form of racism that runs so deep and so naturalized in the American unconscious that it can slip so easily out of the mouth of a pedagogical expert at a public event celebrating education?

The problem with McWhorter's query is that it cannot be asked in a historic vacuum. The problem is that it is *the* question that has always attached itself to, and dismissed, the Asian American subject in American polity. That question has assured the political invisibility of Asian Americans for decades, even during times when they faced brutal consequences from discrimination. My interest is not what should happen to the Purdue chancellor. I want to talk about Asian American lives, and I want to address the yoking and choking relationship between "merit" and "injury" in the game of American racial recognition: the way we quantify and hierarchize injury as a basis for political worthiness.

There is something terribly wrong about the way we think about racial recognition in this country: a crude calculus based on damage. When the news about the wave of anti-AAPI violence first broke in major U.S. media in 2020, I felt a sense of relief alongside the sorrow. Maybe finally, I thought, people will start to take seriously anti-Asian sentiments with the same urgency that they bring to other kinds of racism. But as soon as I thought that, I made myself queasy. Is this what it takes? A political imagination—or, really, lack thereof—that predicates recognition on egregious harm? How many Asian Americans have to be hurt or die before they count in the dialogue about American social justice?

On the scale of American wounding, Asian Americans always come up short, too light to qualify. Implicit behind this calculation is the idea of Asians as "perpetual foreigners," with their incomprehensible, jarring tongues, outside of mainstream culture, and hence a little ribbing is par for the course. Implicit, too, is the shadow of the model minority: Aren't they all doctors and lawyers who are taking more than their fair share of the American pie? So shouldn't we all be "reasonable," in McWhorter's words, in the face of "one tacky joke . . . intended innocently"?

The exhortation for Asian Americans (for presumably Asian Americans are the ones most upset by the Purdue incident) to chill out and not overreact runs the risk, however "innocently intended," of stifling Asian American grief. It corners Asian Americans yet again in their continuously no-win place, a foxhole in a warring racial landscape that supposedly doesn't really include them but that continually, silently (and, at times, not so silently) implicates them. They are doomed to either make the best of or overreact to their own hurtful experiences. Both options perpetuate the injury.

So just how much racism is in question here?

Imagine this: You are an Asian American, perhaps an immigrant who learned English as a second language or perhaps you were born in America and have been speaking English your whole life. Perhaps you're a first gen; perhaps you're not, but your family has made sacrifices so you could be here. Families and friends have traveled far and wide to witness the recognition of your accomplishments. You worked hard to prove yourself to your professor and your peers. And now when you are being conferred the acknowledgment of your labor and worth, the person presenting this honor is making a racist slur as a casual joke at your expense.

We are far from being "long past that kind of thing" (McWhorter). In response to this incident, Stephanie Chang, a state senator in Michigan, told *The Washington Post* that she had gotten "used to hearing this kind of ignorance." The truth is that practically every Asian American person I know, including myself, has experienced some version of this denigration at some point in our life, in our presence, to our face. Sure, most of us just walk away. We don't sue the speaker or track them down at their jobs to demand their resignation. But psychologists have developed a name for this kind of "unintentional," demeaning social interaction: microaggression. Asian Americans are particularly prone to being victims of this, because the modality of Asian American racialization is itself simultaneously ghostly and obdurate, hostile and commonplace. Cathy Park Hong called it a couple of years before this incident: "Pity the Asian accent. It is such a degraded accent, one of the last accents acceptable to mock."

We should not confuse unconscious verbal microaggression with intentional physical harm or with internalized self-denigration, but nor should we fail to recognize their continuities.

When I first read McWhorter's *New York Times* op-ed, I was tempted to ask: If the Purdue chancellor had gone onstage and spoken in a mock minstrel dialect, would McWhorter still have considered that a regrettable faux pas? But I had to pull myself back and reprimand myself for falling into that trap. That kind of comparison is itself harmful and symptomatic, for it is precisely the barometer of *racial injury competition* (who wins the "most injured" contest) that feeds the crisis of interracial sympathies in this country.

The anxiety about "cancel culture" is a red herring. Cancel culture is but a lead-footed response to the helplessness instilled by a system of perverse meritocracy. In fact, cancel culture as such does not exist; there is no organized body of executors issuing red *X*s on people's name cards or rescinding invitations. It is but a facile sound bite created to describe and dismiss a world of hurt, like the "race card." All the more reason why we should not let rhetoric like that distract us from the real conditions of racism and racial recognition in contemporary American life. The real issue at stake is how we make room for our common griefs even as we acknowledge the different modalities and histories of racialization in this country. The real issue is how the invisible cuts of anti-Asian sentiments in the fabric of our everyday lives add up. They can and do manifest themselves as both emotional and physical trauma, a psychic landscape of grief slowly killing us from the inside.

Statistics about Asian American health are hard to come by because Asian Americans are rarely the subject of such research. But new data show that depression among Asian Americans, especially the elderly, has skyrocketed since the beginning of the pandemic. (In January 2023, *Nature* magazine published a study entitled "The Cost of Anti-Asian Racism During the COVID-19 Pandemic" that supplied the quantitative data behind much of what I have been talking about here.) Other studies suggest that Asian Americans, especially young female adults, have the highest rate of suicide deaths of any racial ethnic groups.

So, at elite university campuses, at the very site of Asian American "overachievement," we have, on the one hand, the dismissal and denial of quotidian microaggressions against Asians and Asian Americans, and on the other hand widespread evidence of internal devastation among young Asian Americans.

They may seem unrelated, but they are two sides of a broader phenomenon that we might call Asian pessimism.

By this phrase, I am following Frank Wilderson's influential notion of "Afropessimism." For Wilderson, Afropessimism explicitly holds Blackness as a state of social exclusion/social death. To him, it is more potent and inelastic than any other form of social difference, and so he would likely not appreciate my use of "Asian pessimism." But I make the allusion precisely to resist the logic of and contest over injury. We live in a time of such heightened racial hierarchy that, even as Asian Americans are being bashed and stabbed, they can still be minimized and dismissed as too privileged to count in the stark polarity between Black and white. The racialization of Asian Americans, compounded by xenophobia, has been material and cultural, not always visible but incremental and accretive, a kind of slow violence. The terms and experiences of discrimination and injury play out very differently for Asian Americans because the *modality* of their racialization in America is different from African Americans, but it's crucial that we think through *all forms* of racial deaths and violence in this country. In our ever-fracturing and divided world where antagonism breeds even more trenchant hostility, it's not just the racism but also the tribalism that is killing us.

There's violence on the outside, and then there's violence on the inside.

I put everything on a bagel. Everything, all my hopes and dreams, my old report cards, every breed of dog, every last personal ad on Craigslist, sesame, poppy seed, salt . . . And it collapsed in on itself . . . because when you see you really put everything on your bagel, it becomes this, the Truth: that Nothing Matters.

These words, delivered in a slow monotone, are spoken by an Asian American teenager ironically named Joy (for Joy is anything but joyful) in the 2022 film *Everything Everywhere All at Once,* directed by Daniel Kwan and Daniel Scheinert. Given first the nonexistent, then limited, then compensatory presence of Asian Americans in American cinematic history, it seems bittersweet that the first film with a predominantly Asian cast to gain widespread public recognition, winning multiple awards, including Best Picture at the Oscars, should be this film suffused with the siren song of Asian pessimism and its death drive.

Released on the heels of the pandemic and the tidal wave of anti-Asian violence, *Everything Everywhere,* for all its quirky humor, offers an unrelenting meditation on what happens when estrangement and constant dislocation become the condition of one's daily existence, when one is persecuted by state and family alike, and when one needs to choose between going on or giving in. The mother, Evelyn (Michelle Yeoh), experiences an intergalactic version of what it means to have a target on your back: she is pursued not only by social institutions but also by her angry teenage daughter and her own pessimism. Her daughter, Joy (Stephanie Hsu), possesses and is possessed by a furious, ancient soul named Jobu Tupaki, who embodies, literally, the eternal alien and the alienated.

Young Joy's suicide wish drives the plot and materializes in the story as her "Everything Bagel," a gravitational black hole that threatens to pull Joy and everyone else into its dark, inviting center, an annihilating emptiness where Nothing Matters.

Somehow all her "hopes and dreams" could not forestall, and perhaps even added to, Joy's isolation and disaffection, her profound sense of *not-rightness* in the world and in her own body. It is as if *Everything Everywhere* has taken as its theme the deep anxiety about universal Asian unbelonging that an earlier film like *Crazy Rich Asians* (2018) had secretly fretted over but had repressed under the cover of rampant materialism. (*Crazy Rich Asians'* devouring capitalism, I would argue, is another manifestation of Joy's Everything Bagel.)

I don't know whether the larger public, both those who loved and those who hated *Everything Everywhere,* realizes just how deeply Asian American this film is or why it's useful to see the film's peculiar antics through the specific lenses of Asian American experience. Asian American concerns provide more than an ethnic detail in this story; the film in fact actively references the long history of Asians in America, from the Wang family's laundromat (itself recalling the exclusionary practices that limited Chinese immigrant labor in America) to the Western romance with kung fu mysticism to the notion of the model minority to the figure of the Tiger Mom. And the plot is all about how to navigate and survive the multiplicity of these scripted worlds and roles. Throughout the film, the Daniels (as the codirectors have come to be called) insert understated but biting allusions to this history. In one scene, the rebellious Joy playfully asks a police officer trying to corral her, "Am I not *supposed* to be here, or is it that I *cannot* be here?" This light moment gains weight and becomes acerbic when one hears it as an allusion to and indictment of Asian exclusion in American legal history. This is Joy's arched response to the law and its interpellation.

This goofy, surreal film gets at the deep heart of Asian American not-belonging, of what it is like to be the "perpetual stranger."

For me, the rambunctious humor of the film could not keep the dark message at bay: that to be an immigrant or a hyphenated subject is to live, or die, in a fractured multiverse, one riven with geographic, temporal, and emotional dissonances.

Sitting in that theater, as a teacher and a mother, I couldn't stop thinking about young people who submit to nihilism. The students from my school are exactly the kind of individuals whom others would say "have everything going for them." Yet those young people cannot see a way out of their silent despair, save for an act of such radical self-abandonment. For those students, the possibility and the demand of "everything"—all the expectations of being a model student, of achieving the American Dream, of constantly having to prove themselves worthy to parents, peers, teachers, and themselves—must be crushing even as they spell privilege.

My mind shrinks in fear when I try to imagine how the parents left behind are supposed to survive. How do you bear the unbearable? The mother in the film both does and does not survive. The plot gives us multiple possible outcomes. In one scenario (one alternative universe, in the language of the film), mother and daughter appear as two sentient rocks with stuck-on googly eyes. (Are the googly eyes, by the way, a sly and humorous "correction" to one of the oldest Asian stereotypes in American cinema: the "slanted" Asian eyes?) The ridiculousness of this scene—two rocks telepathically speaking to one another—does nothing to soften the gut punch of the scene. When the smaller Joy-rock throws herself off the cliff, the Evelyn-rock follows, in an act of self-erasure and maternal companionship. At that moment in the film, my heart dropped as well. As a friend's wise mother once said to her when my friend was facing her own demons, "You know what the problem with suicide is? It's contagious."

In another scenario, Evelyn does survive and manages to pull both herself and her daughter back from the dark abyss. Yet she does so not by the physical force of her considerable martial skills or by some grand redemptive gesture, but by finding her way to speak to her daughter with honesty, by saying, yes, the world sucks, and I have not been a perfect mother, nor you a perfect daughter, but "I still prefer to be here with you." This is such a delicate but powerful moment. Imagine the courage it takes not to answer pessimism and violence with the same! Without denying the reality and force of pessimism, the mother reminds the daughter of what it means to possess frail, precious tendrils of familial and loving connections in a world of inevitable griev-ances and disappointments. Even in the fictional world of the film, the possibility of such victory over hopelessness is both tender and tenuous . . . and not at all a guaranteed outcome.

Nihilism, too, is contagious. I used to think of the model minority myth as primarily a socioeconomic concept rather than, say, a medical or psychological one. Indeed, Asian Ameri-cans are more stereotypically associated with being medical caretakers (doctors, nurses, home caregivers) than with being patients themselves. But the model minority has become a pri-mary mental directive for Asian Americans, an expectation that is as silently brutal as it is banal.

I say brutal not because I'm bemoaning the burdens of living up to a supposedly positive stereotype but because the model minority myth exacts an unforgiving health imperative: a narra-tive about an able body that never fails and is capable of constant laboring to achieve. And, of course, none of us are that. Mental and physical limitations *will* confront every one of us. Add the forces of naturalized biases, racism, and xenophobia to the ravages of time, and the Asian American body starts to buckle.

Many of my former students returned to tell me that they hadn't really believed in the "bamboo ceiling" until they graduated and went out into the real world. As high achievers, they had believed in the power of their own agency and determination. It is devastating for Asian Americans, young or old, who are invested in their own abilities and perseverance to discover at some point that all their best intentions, hard work, and good faith might not be sufficient to overcome the barriers of discrimination.

For decades my own scholarship has focused on the invisible damages, what I had called the "hidden grief," of Asian American racial wounding. I had, for instance, written about the unseen psychical costs of assimilation. Here's the irony: the more assimilated you are, the more laborious and invisible the efforts that enabled this ease *and* the more unlikely you are to be cognizant of the psychical energy that has been extracted for this accomplishment. It was not until I found myself embroiled in decades of institution building (believing myself to be a faithful institutional citizen, fighting a good battle for ethnic studies, managing administrative resistance disguised as inert good intentions, bearing the brunt of bureaucratic and interpersonal biases), when my body responded with all kinds of physical disorders, that I realized how truly toxic, not just confounding, Asian American invisibility is. Sooner or later the invisible damages become visible and tangible.

The model minority myth is an insidious identity formation for Asian Americans. It is all the more seductive and dangerous for being tied to that other imaginary reward system, the American Dream. If you put your nose to the grindstone, be a team player, contribute to institutional accretion, and remain gracious in the face of a punch, then surely you will make it, right? And if you don't make it, then it must be because you didn't work hard enough or you weren't good enough rather than because of any systemic inequality or neglect at play. So we have arrived at this double bind: in the face of chronic xenophobic discrimination and political neglect, Asian Americans are hungry for recognition and approval; at the same time, whatever recognition they do receive risks being folded all too quickly back into the model minority/overachiever script that denies Asian American grief in the first place.

At the Academy Awards, Ke Huy Quan, who won Best Supporting Actor for *Everything Everywhere All at Once* and who was himself once a refugee, waved his Oscar statue in the air and shouted with tears in his eyes, "This is the American Dream!" It was genuinely moving to see Asian American artists finally gaining professional recognition after decades of working in the industry, and I do not want to take anything away from Quan and his personal achievements. Yet, it is chilling how quickly that all-devouring narrative of "American Success" asserts itself for the Asian American subject! The seal of the American Dream almost immediately covers over, even as it reactivates, the wounding fetishization of Asian American resilience, of having "grit," of always getting back up after someone knocks you down. Quan himself has spoken elsewhere of the years of depression that dogged him. His exclamation on that stage was even more jarring given how clear-eyed the film is about the deceptive lure of American striving. The Everything Bagel, let us remember, is the Janus face of the American Dream. It's when you put everything in—*all that you own and all that you are*—that you are most at risk.

I want to tell my fellow Asian Americans that Asian American excellence does not do the work that people who tout it want it to do and that representation does not dispel disdain.

Even as we celebrate Asian American aspiration, we must understand it as a form of killing attachment. This is why a note of melancholy ran through that celebratory evening at the Academy of Motion Pictures. In many of the acceptance speeches for this film, one can hear behind the elation the silent roar of decades of personal labor and sacrifice, as well as a haunting sense of invisible others who had come before. When Michelle Yeoh was asked in an interview what it was like to be the first Asian actress nominated for an Oscar, she said simply, "I'm actually not." She must be thinking of previous nominees such as Sessue Hayakawa and Miyoshi Umeki, as well as the countless actors over the decades who played the Generic Asian Man, the Kung Fu Guy, the Pretty Asian Woman, or the Good Servant. There were many ghosts on the stage that night.

I had a vertiginous moment watching that award show. Real life (taking place onstage) handed us a fairy tale of Asian American belonging at the movies that, for all its glitz, is in fact exceptional, specific, and limited. The cinematic fiction that was being awarded, the film itself, on the other hand, eschews realism for fantasy, but embedded within its jagged imagination is a hard kernel of an Asian American unbelonging that is ordinary, undazzling, discordant. It's as if the Oscars show gave us fiction as life, while the movie gave us life as fiction.

Evelyn in the movie—the woman who runs a failing laundry and has to deal with a disappointed father, husband, and daughter, and a woman not to be mistaken with the glamorous actress who performs her—knows that there is no Oscar waiting for her at the end of her day; that's *her* real life. Her hopes are at once more mundane and more ambitious: to hold on to her loved ones in a splintering world.

Postscript

In January 2023, as I was working on the final revisions of this essay and three years into the rise of anti-AAPI violence all across our nation, a friend emailed me the news that an eighteen-year-old student of Asian descent was stabbed seven times in the head by another passenger on a bus in Bloomington, Indiana. The young woman and her attacker were strangers to each other and had no interaction prior to the assault. The perpetrator, a fifty-six-year-old white woman, told officers that she stabbed the victim because the latter appeared "Chinese" and that her own intent was to kill, saying "it would be one less person to blow up our country."

Asian Americans, are we going to survive our one universe? How are we going to navigate the onslaught of, and the temptation to give in to, everything everywhere coming at us all at once? Will we be able to say to our country and to our loved ones that, in spite of all the heartbreaks that have happened to and between us, *I still prefer to be here with you?*

Part V

Good-byes

17

Trip to Disney

I've decided that Disney World is the other Las Vegas, or the Las Vegas for Americans with small children. You get the same unforgiving crowds, the same fanatic showmanship, the same blind craving for "magic!," the same appetite for the exotic-made-local, and, not the least, the same compulsion to have fun no matter how uncomfortable the actual experience might be. Walt Disney was indeed a brilliant businessman. He figured out how to get tens of thousands of people to stand in serpentine queues, all day long, hours at a time, in the burning Florida sun for the joy of a two-minute ride. And this, after having already paid thousands of dollars for the privilege.

Occasionally in the park you might actually see a small child gazing about with genuine wonder, and that's heartwarming, but mostly you see tired and over-caffeinated adults with tired and over-sugared children, more determined than joyous. If Vegas is populated by adults slumped over slot machines and blackjack tables with hollow eyes, Disney is filled with bleary-eyed parents lugging collapsed children. You get kids too big for their strollers hunched over handheld devices; teenagers miming bravado as if they were at Six Flags instead of the Magic Kingdom; sticky-browed little girls with plastic crowns tripping over their polyester princess dresses trying to capture the magic of some dreamed-of femininity, already anticipating an adult woman-hood edged with regret.

I don't mean to sound harsh. It's just that I'd been waiting for an hour and a half in the stifling heat for the Magic Express, which was neither magical nor express, and I was grumpy. There's nothing like Disney World to make you dislike other people's children, or other people, period.

But let's face it, I was one of the crowd. I was there to capture time with my no-longer-small children, one of them about to leave for college in a couple of weeks. Going to Disney in Florida amid a Delta variant surge was undoubtedly not the brightest idea, but the trip had been deferred twice already (first because of my chemo and then because of the first wave of Covid), and I didn't have the heart to disappoint my kids again. Once at the park, my kids kept insisting that I be in the pictures, when it always used to be Mom who took the photos. I wonder whether they, too, feel the preciousness of our time together.

I never experienced Disney as a child. The first time I went I was already a teenager. This was in the late 1970s, and Disney World was relatively new, just as I was still relatively new to America. Disney World, a much bigger enterprise than California's Disneyland, represented but a tiny fraction of the vast Floridian swampland that Walt Disney had purchased. Between 1964 and 1965, the Walt Disney Company created seven companies, including the Reedy Creek Ranch Corporation, Tomahawk Properties, and Latin-American Development and Management Corporation, to purchase 27,400 acres of Florida land from fifty-one landowners. Today the Disney Company owns roughly 30,000 acres in Central Florida; that is, to put it in perspective, eighty times the size of the nation of Monaco and twice the size of Manhattan, a brave new world indeed.

Although my brother and I were no longer children, we nonetheless gave in to the magic. I understood that the whole enterprise was a moneymaking venture (Disney could make an attraction out of its own backstage operations), but I was willing to suspend my disbelief because it was a rare occasion to do precisely that. My regular life was dictated by pragmatic concerns enforced by pragmatic parents. I didn't go to parties because that was unnecessary. I didn't go on the school trip to Paris because that was "extra," and we didn't do extra. But being at Disney gave us all the permission to be distracted, to be susceptible. We marveled at the cheerful cleanliness, the larger-than-life topiaries, the technological innovations, and the romance with futurity. (Remember how cool the Monorail was, especially as it sliced through the center of Disney's Contemporary Resort?) It seemed so American to me, to have this vast place devoted to leisure, play, and unfettered imagination.

I loved, too, the expansiveness of being with Vacation Dad. Vacation Dad was lighthearted, prone to silliness, not penny-pinching, and not judgmental. He ordered appetizers at restaurants and let us buy sentimental souvenirs. He was open to detours and clapped like a child under fireworks. His delight licensed and sweetened our delights.

When I was growing up, my frugal parents did not "do" vacations. Yet, looking back, in those brief years when my brother and I were both in high school, before college, my parents ended up taking us to Disney at least three times. They must have been aware, as I am now with my kids, that opportunities for family trips were quickly slipping away. One of those times we went to Disney as part of a larger Florida road trip where we drove down to the Everglades and the Keys, went on countless jungle cruises, saw mermaids at Weeki Wachee beach, witnessed water ski feats at Cypress Gardens, and discovered by accident the Dalí Museum in St. Petersburg. Who knew one of the largest collections of Dalí's work could be found in Florida, where the aged docent suggested that, when looking at a Dalí, it's best to close one eye?

Everything about that trip was outside of our usual way of doing things, a time-out from our disciplined life. That night in St. Petersburg on an unscheduled stop (itself unusual), we took a moonlit stroll on the beach (equally unusual for my parents). My mother said wistfully that she wished she could lie down on the sand (unimaginable for my very put-together mother) and look at the stars. I told her to turn her back to me. We stood back-to-back, linked arms, and I bent forward so that she could lie on my back while looking up into the night sky. We stayed like that for as long as I could hold the pose.

This time around with my kids, Disney itself seemed engaged in an elaborate exercise in nostalgia. For all the talents and corporate funds at its disposal, Disney World had remained curiously or willfully un-updated since its inception in 1971, exactly a year before we emigrated from Taiwan. And the rides had not fared well over time. These days Tomorrowland would be more aptly called "Retro Land," and the Carousel of Progress more of a time capsule. Walt Disney used to be known for his extravagant penchant for futuristic visions, but Disney World today looked backward rather than forward. Perhaps it always did.

Disney World was, after all, erected as a larger copy of Disney-land, which had its origins in the mid-1950s.

Even when a particular future technological invention being showcased had still yet to be realized in practice, the vision itself testified more to the past than the future. Today's Tomorrowland showcased a vision of a slim woman in the future, sitting in a chair with her head improbably covered by a giant silver dome resembling an oversize salon dryer. A diagram demonstrated what was presumably going on inside the dome: a mechanical hand brushing out strands of hair while others placed curlers in other strands, wielded hairspray, plucked the woman's eye-brows, and so on. Although today we do not yet have such a one-stop, hands-free device at our disposal, the vision exudes a 1950s aura, if only because women no longer groom themselves in exactly this way anymore. Our visions of the future always bear the time stamp of the present and, in this way, are always already dated. (Is this why I'm always a little disappointed by science fiction, which in all its attempts to be imaginative often ends up recapitulating our current moment anyway?) We look to the future to find our past dreams.

My dad used to be inordinately charmed by It's a Small World, but then, being an ob-gyn, he was always fond of small human beings, the smaller the better. I often thought my gravest sin, in my father's eyes, was that I grew up. It's a Small World made no such mistake. It stayed stubbornly "small" in the face of time, its harem of never-aging children still singing with relentless, repetitive cheer their messages about world diversity and unity through the narrowest, most clichéd terms available: Holland = wooden shoes; China = slanted-eyed dolls; Mexico = fiestas.

As much as I tried to call up and relive my dad's delight,

and even my own past enjoyments at Disney World, this time I just couldn't suspend the critical me. Is this the inevitable outcome of earned wisdom or just age? All the blinking signage around Disney, on buildings, walls, and buses—*"Fill Up on the Pixie Dust!"* *"Get Your Magic On!"* *"Never Lose the Magic!"*—bore down on me like reprimands or subliminal exhortations designed to prevent grown-ups from stalking off in impatience.

Then there was that dissonant conjunction of the global and the provincial that haunted almost every Disney venture and was most euphorically proclaimed at EPCOT (Experimental Prototype Community of Tomorrow), which expanded that paradoxically mono-multicultural logic tenfold. That is, Disney cosmopolitanism operated by restaging internationalism as parochialism. Disney France predictably offered croissants and a mini Eiffel Tower, while Disney China hawked fans and triangular bamboo rice hats. The racial imaginary underpinning Disney's cosmopolitan vision was stuck in the 1950s. But then maybe so is the American racial imaginary today. Frankly, it was more than a little disconcerting to witness so many white people casually walking about wearing coolie hats in 2021.

When EPCOT first opened in 1982—the same year, by the way, that *Blade Runner* came out—the idea that you could go "off world" and magically simulate visiting twelve countries in the same space and time might have held some piquant charm, but today, given the relative affordability of air travel (certainly if you can afford Disney, you can fly to Europe), the global circulation of goods, the expanding diaspora, not to mention the internet, the world has become much smaller, making the exoticized and miniaturized world of EPCOT less than experimental, hardly worldly, and singularly American.

Why spend all that money and effort to stand in line to see

a small imitation Eiffel Tower when one could see the real one for probably less money, if not less of a crowd? It must have something to do with the fantasy of bringing the world into your backyard, of sampling an entertaining *foreign Other* while you get to stay within the safety of American borders. It's a fundamentally imperial view: the world spread out for your gaze and sampling. At least when it first opened, EPCOT tried to put on some gestures of internationalism, so that if you were a foreigner in the United States, going to EPCOT might give you a little nostalgic sense of imagined homecoming. Disney used to boast of hiring foreign nationals to staff EPCOT, and back then you could hear foreign languages being spoken among the people who worked there. This time, the two foreign words we heard from the staff on the entire trip were *Bienvenue!* and *Hola!* It is as if Disney had given up on the ambition of an international community and was now resigned to catering mainly to untraveled Americans. This same logic extended to almost all of Disney's new parks in the 1980s and '90s. Animal Kingdom, for instance, basically turned out to be "Africa" and "Asia": the former populated with huts and a five-minute safari, the latter decorated with ramshackle villages and signs in designer broken English ("Me Out to Lunch. Be Light Back") . . . in short, Animal Kingdom *was* the third world as imagined by the West.

It didn't help that Florida was, during our trip, a hot spot for Covid transmission. My autoimmune system was still pretty shot, and I was terrified for my life the entire time. Although masks were required at all rides and attractions, one out of three people took their masks off or wore them improperly the moment they passed a "cast member" checkpoint. And although public signs all around advised social distancing, people squeezed in no matter how far we retreated, standing shoulder to shoulder as though such proximity would somehow speed up the lines. I kept thinking I would be pretty damn upset if, after all the cancer treatments and months of quarantine, I ended up catching Covid in Disney World, of all places.

Once on this trip I audibly gasped and ran like a coward the other way—when a sea of huffing, unmasked people surged toward us as they rushed to the opening of a particularly popular new attraction—but mostly I was able to keep my anxiety and ill humor in check. We were there to celebrate our family time. I didn't want to take away my kids' chance to be children again for a bit before the world called them away. My daughter was scheduled to move out of the house and into her college dorm a week after we got back. I had been packing for that for weeks . . . well, really for years. Seven years ago I bought her a comforter for college that I recently unwrapped. Thirteen years ago I framed two identical sets of photo booth pictures of the two of us giggling. My thought was that I would keep one and give her the other when she went away to school. I pull those out of the closet. I can't see her future. Mostly what I see is that giggling little girl in my arms . . . and the countless dreams vested in her.

During our seven-day stay in Disney, my daughter walked about, seemingly oblivious to the sun and the long lines, light as a lark, holding my hand everywhere we went: walking, waiting, eating. Was this the same girl who both broke my heart and made me proud when she walked ahead of me toward her new daycare without looking back? The same girl who would later go on thrill rides of all kinds without fear while I stayed behind on the ground? Was her carefree bliss now real or at least partially a show for me? Was she performing the invisible labor of joy for me, the way I did for her, and my parents for me? Under the oppressive weight of the hot sun, were my daughter and I imprinting memories for one another the way that my parents and I did so long ago?

I had my hand in my daughter's. I wanted to hang on forever, and I wanted to tell her to let go and move ahead.

18

Passing Vignettes

The pharmacy in my grandfather's home medical practice in the city of Tainan sat in the middle of the front part of his house immediately facing the entrance hall, which doubled as the waiting room. The dispensary stood as a self-contained structure, like a secret room, walled off from the rest of the house by tall mahogany panels and its own wood ceiling. Narrow transoms lined the top of the tall room to allow light into this inner space. The only apertures were the door and a little window with a ledge where the nurses used to dispense the medication that my grandfather ordered.

By the time I knew this room, it had long been decommissioned. My grandfather retired in his mid-forties, which is probably why he lived to age ninety-nine even though he smoked, was allergic to vegetables, and ate bacon every morning of his life. By the time I played in the room, all the drugs had been removed, but my grandfather had left untouched most of his old tools. On the table ledge that ran around the room sat all kinds of cool objects: brown glass bottles tall and short, skinny and fat, each serenely topped with matching glass stoppers; marble mortars and pestles that you could grind almost anything in; miniature spatulas, skinny-headed spoons, and pinchers of every size lined up like tiny soldiers on ivory trays; a pill grinder and counter I'd repurposed for abusing and counting jelly beans; balance scales accompanied by wooden boxes that opened to reveal tiny silver cylindrical weights in ascending order, each encased in its own perfectly contoured dugouts. Whenever I pulled one out or put one back, I could feel the seamless glide of metal against wood and could almost hear a sighing *swish*. I'm pretty sure this room first taught me the deep pleasures of compulsive organization, the security and virtue of everything having its place.

But the best part of the room was the row after row of vertically stacked small wooden drawers that lined the walls from table height all the way up to the transoms. There were hundreds of these mini drawers, or so it seemed to me, each about five inches wide and three inches tall, with mini brass curved handles under which you hooked your index finger, like a card catalog. My mother said there used to be a rolling ladder to reach the top drawers where the medications were kept. I loved cloistering myself in that skinny vertical room. I imagined all the powders and pills, all the colors and shapes of forbidden things, inside all those dark, miniature spaces.

•   •   •

In the privacy of couples therapy, the man pleaded, *Please, if I can't make it with you, I can't make it with anyone.* Then, another tack, *I'm your last chance. If you leave me now, you will never get to have the children or family you always wanted.*

That did it. The woman who was always weighed down by insecurity lifted her head and thought, *Probably, but I'd rather bet on myself.*

•   •   •

At a reception in honor of a distinguished visiting Chinese intellectual who had come all the way from Beijing, the wife of an
equally prominent American scholar said to the elderly guest
of honor, "Asian people just don't seem to age! You all look so
youthful. We must all look so old to you!" The woman laughed
charmingly. Given Chinese politeness and all, she must have
expected the scholar to demur or at least reassure her that she
certainly didn't look old.

The older man looked impassive, grave, and seemed to be
searching for an answer. Perhaps he didn't fully comprehend her
English. Finally, he said, "Mm . . . yes." It was not clear to those
listening to what the gentleman was assenting.

•   •   •

In the 1940s, my maternal grandfather, whom I adored, was at
the prime of his life. A patriarch and a tyrant, he was the first
doctor trained in Western medicine in Tainan and supported his
own household and several members of the extended family. He
ruled his family, his nurses, and his patients with an iron hand.
He had his medical practice at the front of his house, equipped
with his own drug dispensary, two or three nurses, and a single
examination room. The patients sat in the large foyer that served
as the waiting room, some with bags of oranges, some with
homemade baos for the doctor. He would keep them waiting
while he leisurely ate his breakfast or lunch in the private part
of the house while my grandmother stood anxiously by, softly
reminding him that people were waiting. He always said in the

years that followed that a major reason he lived such a long life was because he was a patient man.

•   •   •

As a young assistant professor, I was paired with a senior colleague in the department's new buddy system, designed to support junior faculty. One day this man called me into his office to say, "You rarely come to see me. You know I'm supposed to be your buddy, right? Is there anything that you want to share with me, anything at all?" When I said I was doing well, he pushed, "Tell me honestly, there must be something that's not going so well?"

So I said I did find the large institutional environment a little isolating. Our department didn't have a lounge so I rarely saw my new colleagues except by the mailboxes, where no one was inclined to linger. He listened, started to sort through his mail, and told me the story of how, as an assistant professor, his first book manuscript, now a foundational text that had launched a new critical school of thought, was actually rejected six times before it was finally accepted. He said, "I took every one of those rejection letters and stuffed them inside my desk drawer and never said anything to my senior colleagues about them." He finally looked up to meet my gaze and said, "People only back winners."

Later when I fumed to a friend about what felt like a setup, my friend said, "That was kind of an asshole thing to do. But, look at it this way, he really did teach you something about professionalism as he understood it. In a way, he *was* mentoring you." It's true; I never forgot the lesson.

•   •   •

At a strategic meeting about how to revitalize the future of the humanities on campus, the proposal that emerged and excited my colleagues from across the campus the most was that the university open a bar at the faculty club so that colleagues might gather after work, relax, and enjoy a cocktail or two before dinner. That's when real conversations and ideas happen, someone said, when real decisions can be made. One of two women and the only woman of color on the committee, I pointed out that those hours coincided with some of the busiest times for colleagues with child-care responsibilities, which happened to be women most of the time, and that the proposal might effectively reproduce the old boys' club.

After the meeting, as I was gathering up my things to go pick up my kids—their school started charging double the after-school fees after six p.m. and, if I were late, that would keep the teachers from getting home in time for their own families—one of the senior male colleagues said to me, "Wow, Anne, I wouldn't have guessed it, but you argue like a man." I don't think he meant it as a compliment.

•   •   •

Some hard truths:

When you're the only Asian person in the room, whether it is a room full of white people or full of other persons of color, you are either the pet (good for demonstration) or the intruder.

I feel in my bones the importance and urgency of the human-

ities and the arts in a world of increasing inhumanity and neoliberal expediency. But my bones do not match the world.

Say it. *No one likes you.*

•   •   •

I went to an inaugural meeting for Asian and Asian American
staff at the university, convened, I gathered, in response to the
rise in violence against people of Asian descent. I was thrilled to
see all the different faces in that virtual meeting room. I saw in
action how global and ethnically diverse the category of "Asian
America" is, an assertion and a disclaimer that every Asian
American studies professor feels obliged to rehearse. But a few
minutes into the conversation, even as people warmed to our
newfound solidarity, strands of ever-finer distinctions within
groups and subgroups started to emerge: ethnic and national
differences, Asian versus Southeast Asian, Chinese versus Taiwanese, American born versus immigrant, recent immigrants
versus old immigrants, and more. Someone complained of how
a false perception of Asian passivity holds Asian Americans back
from being considered for leadership positions. Someone else
piped up to agree but thought that Americans should value
Asian modesty and self-effacement. Someone said we *are* Americans, and someone said we ought to be more Asian. It felt a little
like witnessing a Tower of Babel but where no one realized they
were talking in a different language. By the end of the meeting, I
had decided not to attend another one of these meetings.

"Asianness" in America is Penelope patiently weaving and
unraveling the tapestry, waiting for a homecoming that may or
may not be wished for.

.   .   .

Right next door to my grandfather's internal medicine practice and its Western-style pharmacy sat a traditional Chinese
medicine shop whose real name few remembered because it
was largely known by the locals as the Golden Statue. The two
neighbors could not have been more different: one was a bastion
of Western modernity, the other a staple of Eastern tradition-
alism. My grandfather's building exuded restrained authority, a
three-story building with an impassive facade of white stone and
glass. Save for the elegant inscription "Yeh Family Internal Medicine" that ran across the balustrade off the second-floor balcony
that you could only see from across the street, a pedestrian could
be forgiven for thinking it was only a private residence. The
herb shop next door, on the other hand, was only one story tall
but announced itself loudly: an open, bustling shop into which
you could easily look as you pass by. The store had no written
signage, only the large, eponymous Golden Statue, looking half
Buddha, half vagrant, a figurine to which I was always drawn to
and repelled by at the same time, standing on a pedestal at the
front and center of the store.

There was a time when practically everyone in the city of
Tainan knew who my grandfather was. Dr. Yeh Chok-chiu was
celebrated as much for his modern Western skills and unerring
diagnosis as for his sternness. He was known to have no qualms
about yelling at his patients, especially when they failed to follow instructions. And everyone knew the Golden Statue, too,
which had stood in the same spot for over two hundred years.

Few people, however, knew that my grandfather and his com-
petitor next door were cousins. I called the latter Great-Uncle #8,
because all the cousins in the extended family were numbered

Golden Statue Herbal Medicine
Store, Tainan, Taiwan

Yeh Family Internal Medicine,
c. 1967, Tainan, Taiwan

in order of age. (My grandfather was, of course, #1, being the eldest.) And even fewer knew that they were, in fact, biological brothers. Great-Uncle #8 was my grandfather's younger brother, who had been "given away" by his father, my great-grandfather, to his wife's brother, who didn't have a son to carry on his family name. The biological brothers grew up as cousins in the same family compound, as extended families did then, with different last names and different parents but playing and eating most meals together.

As a child, I found the story distressing. I always felt sad for Great-Uncle #8. The intimacy of such coexisting, extended families must have been a source of both comfort and alienation. What was it like to live next to and grow up alongside people you knew were your real parents and brother, but were no longer? What was it like to be the one not kept?

My mother explained that people of a certain class and generation often did things like that back then to "keep it all within the family." This way my great-uncle got to inherit as the older son of the Chun family, while my grandfather remained the oldest inheriting Yeh son. And although the brothers/cousins ended up in different walks of life, they shared a similar legacy. The Yeh family has always been in the healing business. My great-great-great-grandfather was a scholar who studied Chinese medicine. When he first opened the herb store, he worried that those who were illiterate wouldn't be able to read the sign on the store, so he adopted the Golden Statue, modeled after a well-known Good Samaritan in folklore, as the store mascot, and stuck it outside as a visual marker. My great-grandfather, also a scholar and an Anglophile, sent his firstborn son, my grandfather, to train in Western medicine because he thought that was the future. But he gave his younger son (who became his nephew) the run of the old family business. So, my mother concluded, both sons stood to gain. But I still wasn't so sure the inheritance was worth it.

•   •   •

Whether on an overnight trip to New York or for a month's stay in Paris, I carry the same small, packed-to-the-brim, carry-on luggage. In one context, I look like a spoiled princess; in another, a seasoned nomad.

•   •   •

At my first teaching job, a colleague and I met up on the snowy sidewalk on our way to the campus. We paused to look at the glistening bare tree limbs, each in its own icy sheath. We were in front of a store window displaying snow globes of all sizes. Through the glass, I pointed out all the ones with the bubbles on top, the ones where the water had started to evaporate. I thought those added horizon to the scenes inside. My friend said, "Those bubbles always make me think that the people inside are drowning."

•   •   •

Another friend and I walked through a department store. As we passed the cosmetic counter, the saleswoman stepped in front of us, blocking our progress. "Have you tried our new perfume?" she asked brightly. When we demurred, she did not give up. She pointed to the display on the counter, a well-organized presentation of bottles in pastel hues, neatly numbered 1, 2, and 3, and asked, "Are you aware of our system?"

My friend replied without missing a beat, "Yes . . . it's called capitalism."

．　　　．　　　．

When I applied to college, my CV said I had all the "leadership" qualities required for future success: editor of the yearbook, editor of the school literary magazine, Science Student of the Year, a state championship debater. My records showed a well-rounded go-getter with a passion for winning. But the truth was more humbling: it was the teachers who sought me out, who courted, coaxed, and cultivated me into these positions. I did my jobs well, even ended up thriving, but I lacked the exact thing that the category really meant to capture: the killer instinct, the ambition to seek the center stage.

All through my teen years, my secret fear: if my teachers were not prodding me, and if I were not prodding myself, then my true hidden turtle would take over. This is the kind of thinking that leads to failure and that I have to guard against: the desire to bury my head in my shell, bake in the sun, do nothing.

．　　　．　　　．

Sometimes, patients from my grandfather's medical practice would sneak over to the Golden Statue next door with their diagnosis and seek my great-uncle the herbalist's counsel. (That's when my grandfather would yell.) But I, too, loved sneaking over to the Golden Statue. I could get to it from one of the inner courtyards in my grandfather's house. All I had to do was cross the garden with the stone benches, jump over the old water gully that ran between the two buildings, and cross another small courtyard before popping into the back entrance of the Golden Statue.

It always took a moment for my eyes to adjust to the dimness in the store. The herbs didn't like a lot of sunlight. Where my grandfather was circumspect and disciplined, my great-uncle was jolly and relaxed. He often didn't show up at the store until two or three in the afternoon. His wife, Great-Aunt #8, on the other hand, was there at the store every day, all day long. I liked Great-Aunt #8 a lot. Unlike my grandmother, who was frank about her preference for boys, my great-aunt told me she loved little girls and that I could always come visit.

She knew that I came for the row of paper squares hanging on the back wall, tacked by the corners so each square stack looked diamond shaped, in descending order by size. They went from about 8 by 8 centimeters to 30 by 30. My great-aunt and great-uncle used the papers to fold up dry preparations, and they would write instructions right on the packages. Those squares made the best origami paper: they had enough body to withstand manipulation but were thin and flexible enough to make the most intricate folds. With both a glossy side and a matte one, they also made excellent drawing paper, fully adaptive to crayons, pencils, and markers alike. I would spend hours on a stool in the store, folding or drawing, until my mother located me and dragged me away.

I was told not to go over to the Golden Statue because my great-aunt and great-uncle had a business to run and I would get in the way. Besides, how would it look for Dr. Yeh's grandchildren to be seen hanging out in the Chinese medicine store? I never told my grandfather that what he feared was actually happening: that my great-uncle or great-aunt would display my brother and me to their clients as living advertisements of happy, healthy kids who grew up on Chinese herbal supplements, which, of course, we did not.

•   •   •

When I asked why Great-Uncle #8 wasn't always in the store regularly, I was told he liked to sleep a lot and that, when he slept, no one could rouse him. I imagined he was kind of like that American story of the man who slept for twenty years. Years later, I would come to learn that Great-Uncle #8 suffered from depression and would sometimes spend days in bed without moving. But when he was up and in the store, he was a ball of energy. He knew every client by name and often the names of their children and parents. And if he caught sight of my brother and me, he would abandon the store to others and take turns piggybacking us across the street to his house, where he let us watch television, which my grandfather disapproved of.

As a child, I was always puzzled by the relationship between my grandfather and his brother/cousin. They lived across the street from each other and worked next door to each other. The women in the families shared cooking recipes, gossip, and sewing projects. But I don't think I remember ever seeing the brothers/cousins hanging out together alone. My grandfather stood tall with his iron-rod back and his elegant pipe always in hand. My great-uncle stooped, as if he spent his life bending over a counter. My grandfather was decisive, my great-uncle soft-spoken. My grandfather was openly dismissive of Chinese medicine. It's old-fashioned and not real medicine, he would say. He was critical of Great-Uncle #8's lackadaisical attitude and lack of ambition. I could never see the brothers in them.

My grandfather retired early, in his forties. One day he closed up shop and started to travel with my grandmother. Great-Uncle #8 and his wife continued to run their store. Over the years the Golden Statue remained the most popular herbal medicine store in town, competitive with all the newfangled Western drugstores. Loyal clients swore by its prescriptions, calling them miraculous, and believed in them with a fervor that seemed almost mystical. Decades later, in America and when I was much older, my mother told me that she suspected that Great-Uncle #8 must have sneaked small amounts of powdered aspirin or antibiotics into his preparations. I do not know if that was the truth or a sign of her inherited bias. If it were true, I wonder whether Great-Uncle #8 stole the Western medicine from my grandfather or whether the latter willingly gave them to his younger brother.

•   •   •

Last night at the outdoor dance held by the local library in our little town, my husband and I started a conga line. Well, he started and I followed. As usual, he's the Pied Piper and I the self-conscious, embarrassed one pulled into the fun.

Afterward, I thanked him for taking the lead. It was a blast how many strangers our line managed to pick up. I would never have the courage to start something like that in public. He said to me, "Do you know who the most important person in a conga line is? The first follower."

•   •   •

As a young man, my grandfather loved to dance. At the bottom of his closet, he kept two rows of dance shoes that my grandmother carefully polished; if she was too busy, she had one of the servants do it. When my mother was still a child, my grandfather converted the top floor of his home into a dance room with polished cherry-wood floors and a gramophone, one of the first privately owned record players in the city. Every Saturday night he held a dance party to which he invited all of his male friends and for which he hired professionals from the local dance hall as their partners. (Dancing was not for respectable wives.) His personal favorite was a woman who called herself Ruby. Years later when I heard this story, I marveled at how a young woman in Tainan who hadn't traveled much and who didn't speak English nonetheless managed to pick the gaudiest name in the English language.

My mother recalled that those were exciting days for the entire household. She remembered, not because she got to participate, but because the preparation would start early in the morning and last all day. On those days her mother would have little time for her, especially once the guests started to arrive in the evening. My mother, then five or six, would hide under the stairwell to watch the men go up the steps with their shining shoes and crisp pant legs. None of them, she thought, wore their Western suits with the natural ease of her father. All night long her mother, my grandmother, would be busy supervising the drinks and the ceaseless flow of cold and warm plates being carried up and down the flights of stairs. The long kitchen was at the back of the house on the first floor, while the parties were at the front on the third floor. My grandmother personally accompanied the servants with each delivery but always stopped short at the landing.

On nights when the parties went too long into the early hours of the morning, my grandmother would wake up my mother

Author's mother as a child, sitting between her parents

and send her upstairs to ask her father to wind up the party and come back downstairs.

.   .   .

My husband watches *Game of Thrones,* which I cannot bear.

I watch *Succession,* which my husband cannot bear.

They're really the same story, except one is set in an imagined past and the other in contemporary American corporate culture. The difference is that my husband has a high tolerance for physical violence and none for emotional violence, while I am clearly the opposite.

.   .   .

My daughter had been what people called a colicky baby, a way of saying the adults never figured it out what was wrong. The warning sign: her mouth would open wide, contort silently into an impossible little square, pause, and then out would come a hair-raising wail, the kind that reached deep down into your gullet and yanked your soul right out.

She didn't sleep through the night until she was three years old. She had night terrors that terrorized us. I was so sleep deprived that I walked into a wall in my own house and chipped a tooth. Once she cried so hard and for so long—nearly four hours of nonstop distress (how can such small lungs produce so many decibels for so long?)—that I called the pediatrician in panic. I had tried everything: changed her diaper, fed her (or tried to), burped, walked, rocked, sang, and then did it all over again . . . to no avail. Surely she was getting dehydrated. I saw my neighbor peer out of her window, probably wondering what evil was being done to an innocent infant.

The pediatrician didn't want me to drive considering the condition of the baby, whom she could hear in the background. She called an ambulance to pick us up. But a nearby fire truck with an EMT showed up instead. When the loud and long fire engine pulled up in front of our little house, rattling our windowpanes, a huge burly firefighter in full gear got out and walked up the driveway to our front door, where I stood with my daughter. I thought, oh great, now the baby is really going to freak out. As the giant shadow of the man approached, my daughter stopped abruptly, opened her wet shining eyes even wider, and smiled at the stranger. He looked at me (with slight annoyance? with pity?) and said, "Ma'am, she looks fine to me."

•   •   •

Have you ever noticed that breast pumps can talk?

My first machine spoke Taiwanese: *Bird-in-nest, bird-in-nest, bird-in-nest . . .*

My second spoke English: *Shush-the-gun, shush-the-gun, shush-the-gun . . .*

My third spoke Cat: *Mium, mium, mium . . .*

•   •   •

Living in the Bay Area in Northern California taught me everything I knew about food, in fact, taught me to *think* about food beyond mere sustenance. Prior to California, I didn't know how to debone sand dabs or that figs go with prosciutto or that there were purple potatoes or thirty different kinds of apples or giant green bean pods that hold bright white beans inside dotted with hot pink spots like mini dinosaur eggs.

One night a friend with whom I had been flirting took me to a small, elegant, very quietly chic Californian restaurant on the border of Berkeley and Oakland. One of the desserts the waitress recited from memory was an apple galette. I asked, "What is a galette?" The server said, "It is a profound tart." My friend raised one eyebrow at me. I looked at him and asked, "Who is she calling profound?"

·　　·　　·

In *The Pillow Book,* Lady Sei Shōnagon pronounced that "Babies should be fat, but oxen should have narrow foreheads."

She's not wrong.

·　　·　　·

I have never thought of myself as beautiful, had in truth mourned that I was not, but I realize now that I had the beauty of youth. There's no young face that doesn't have some beauty to it. I wish my younger self could have known this and enjoyed this gift.

I wish I had worn a bikini every day of my life when I was in my twenties. Perhaps even my thirties, too.

·　　·　　·

There was this song that my mother and I both loved when we lived in our flat in Taipei. The lyrics were essentially about nostalgia and regret, the stuff of popular songs, about how the past can never return and that it can only be relived or relished as things that are no longer. I used to sing this song nonstop and especially loudly in the shower. It made my mother laugh, because who's ever heard of a seven-year-old mourning regret?

After we moved to the U.S. and I stopped reading Chinese books, my mother and I continued to sing this song for a while: at the top of our voices, in the car going to Atlanta, to Hilton Head, to Charleston. Over time, the lyrics faded, but the tune stayed in my head. I never thought I could find this song again. I didn't know who the singer was nor did I have a recording of the song. I could barely write the title in Mandarin. But yesterday I decided to trust the miracle of the internet, typed in various English combinations of the words "Taiwanese song things past regret no return" and, amazingly, the song popped up on You-Tube! There it was: 往事只能回味 (*Wǎng shì zhǐ néng huí wèi*), this version sung by You Ya, released in 1970. Just listening to the intro brought the song back in all its fullness. *Every word came back.* Suddenly, I was a native speaker again, a child bred on the melancholy of 1970s Taiwanese pop music.

I sent my mother the link in excitement. She didn't know how to work the link. I called her on the phone and played the song to her, holding the receiver up to my computer speaker. Afterward, I got back on the phone and asked, "Can you believe it? We found it!"

My mother said, "I don't know that song. I have never heard of it."

•   •   •

When I finished my first book, I sent a hard copy of the manuscript to my father. It was an academic study about literary theory, law, and race politics. I didn't expect him to read it, but I felt obliged to show him what I had been working on for the past seven years. A small part of me feared that he might actually read it. Would he belittle my labor? Would he see some shadows of us behind the scholarship?

He didn't acknowledge receiving the package, but two weeks later I got my manuscript back, all marked up, with a note attached: "I have no idea what you're talking about, but here're all the typos and grammar mistakes that I could find."

And, indeed, he had gone through every word, every sentence, and every page of this four-hundred-page manuscript that he did not understand.

·   ·   ·

My mother started ballroom dancing lessons in her fifties. There was no way that my dad was going to join her. But almost a decade after she started, when he was sixty-seven and two years short of retirement, he agreed to learn the waltz for my wedding.

Who'd have thought that this bookworm of a man who had no hobbies except reading scientific journals, who was so shy and solitary that he often sat in the corner reading a book during social gatherings, at least during American parties, who disliked drawing attention to himself, should become such a ballroom enthusiast? He and my mom started going dancing every week. He bought videocassettes to study. He took copious notes after classes. (Who takes notes from dance lessons? Someone who had developed his own system of mysterious notations and drawings.) My parents, who rarely traveled because that is a frivolous way to spend money, started going on trips and cruises and danced the nights away. Once, at some medical convention where I went to join them, I saw him stand up and ask a stranger, a white woman, across the large round table to dance. *Okay, who are you, and what have you done with my father?* He was like a new person. Dancing did more to put my father at ease in America than decades of living there and enjoying professional success.

Just shy of a year after I waltzed with my dad at my first wedding, I applied for a divorce. This turned my view of myself upside down. The extent to which I had let myself down made getting up each morning an insurmountable chore. Every morning I considered how I could manage to stay in bed all day, what excuses I could give people, all the while knowing the thinking was buying me more time in bed. The very prospect of getting up to brush my teeth and get dressed exhausted me. I was never suicidal, but I thought a lot about the concept and thought I understood why people do it. That summer I took a couple of weeks to go home to my parents, a last-ditch survival instinct, to have someone else take the burden of feeding me. I spent most of my time there in bed, too. My parents forced me to go to one of their dance parties. I sat in the corner, small and numb. My parents looked like strangers to me across the room, laughing and moving in a crowd of white southerners, holding each other, learning new choreographies.

Back in San Francisco, I joined the YMCA and started salsa lessons.

·　　·　　·

When, in the name of progress in the late 1990s, the city of Tainan decided to widen its streets, it offered my grandfather a nominal fee and tore down the front third of his house, destroying what used to be his medical practice and all the spaces within. There's no longer a whole, physical building halfway across the world that anchors the substance, holds the weight, of my dreams.

I miss my grandfather's old dispensary, with its slightly old medicinal smell, its pristine and by-my-time-useless order, and its abandoned mysteries. As a small child I would spend hours just opening and closing as many of the mini drawers in the room as I could reach. Some of the lower shelves still held goodies, miniature bottles and stoppers, organized by shapes and sizes. My mom told me that, during our summer visits and before I could walk or climb the wooden stools to play in that room, she used to feed me in my high chair there. All she had to do was to pull out a drawer and put it in front of me and I would be wholly occupied by its contents, making mealtime a cinch.

Years later, with my own children in America, I collected in a plastic shoebox container a bunch of old cosmetic bottles and cases of various sizes and shapes, some clear glass, some frosted, some in enticing colors, some with lids that screwed on, some with satisfying snaps, and some with squeezy tops, each piece a puzzle for chubby little fingers to take apart and restore. That box entertained my kids longer than many toys did. But I do feel sorry for my children that I had a whole apothecary to myself while they had a Sterilite box.

19

How I Keep Losing My Father

1. The Toast

Few people in my life today know that I was previously married: a short, disastrous marriage that I couldn't even blame on youthful infatuation. I was already in my mid-thirties. I thought I was being clear-eyed about the right thing to do.

My parents were uncharacteristically un-opinionated about my engagement even though they'd been pressing me to get married since I turned eighteen. During college, unbeknownst to me, my parents used to send pictures of me to my father's Táidà Medical School friends, most of whom are expats in the U.S. and had sons in Ivy League medical schools. I used to get random invitations from young men I didn't know who claimed to be family friends and who happened to be in town. By the time I reached my thirties, my parents had given up on the dream of my marrying a Taiwanese surgeon. At that point, I had been downgraded: *anyone,* please.

I believed in the myth of my resistance to their expectations for so long that I couldn't see when I gave in. The shameful truth, somewhere deep where I didn't want to look, was that I knew I didn't love this person, not in the right way. The even more deeply shameful thing to me was that the me back then would have stayed in that marriage had he turned out to be the good person I believed he was.

That wedding took place in a little old chapel by San Francisco Bay. During the wedding, an old friend's baby started bawling in the audience. I secretly winced, not because I minded but because I knew my new husband would be upset with me later. He had a thing about people who bring uninvited infants to weddings. The reception was held at a celebrated vegetarian restaurant by the water, even though neither of us was a vegetarian, even though picking a vegetarian restaurant was a wholly eccentric choice from my Taiwanese parents' point of view. There in the gorgeous restaurant, full of people I barely knew, my normally taciturn father stood up and gave a surprisingly urbane and extended toast with such sharp, dry humor about the impracticality of my chosen career and all the ways in which he had given up on my ability to catch a husband that he had the crowd, including my new husband, doubling over with laughter . . . except my two oldest and dearest friends, who turned to look at me with uneasy eyes.

Behind my smile, in that beautifully lit restaurant by the sea, I thought, *I am being roasted, at my wedding, by my father.*

Eleven months later, I had to call him with the news. I would be the first person in my family, immediate or extended, on either side of the Pacific, to get a divorce. Would he say I told you so even though he hadn't, or you will shame us, or you were always difficult to live with, or you better stick it out? Such deep failure on my part. After a brief silence on the end of the phone across the country, he said, "It can take a lifetime to get to know another person. When one makes a mistake, it is better to correct it." Relief and gratitude flooded my body.

Then he added, "But then, you always did have to learn things the hard way."

2. PICASSO

It was the fall of 1980. My father had a medical meeting in New York City, and he agreed to bring me, a junior in high school, along with him and my mom. My parents usually did these kinds of trips by themselves alone, as close to vacations as they were likely to take. I begged to come along. This would be my first time in Manhattan, and my grand ambition was to see the big Picasso retrospective at the Museum of Modern Art. My dad was dismissive and made fun of my interests in modern art. What did I know about art anyway; why did I waste his money and time on scribbles that a child could do? Once in the city, though, I managed to drag my parents by MoMA. My heart sank at the sight of the line around the block. No way, my father said.

The next morning I woke up in the hotel to find my father already gone. My mom told me he had gotten up early to go wait in line at MoMA. Two hours later he returned with a museum membership and a copy of the exhibition catalog. It turned out the museum had sold out for the day, so he joined the museum in order to obtain a member's admission. To my shocked face, he said, "Well, it was a better deal. You get admission and a free catalog, and that alone is $75."

3. MAPS

After a couple of years of silence, my father came to me one night and told me that he had been living in Colorado, as if he hadn't died. I have never been to Colorado. What was he doing there? The mountains there, he explained, were remarkably green and the air pure. I asked if he could stay for a while or whether I could write to him. He said no, his eyes soft and bland.

Really, Colorado? Is this the best my sad little mind can do? Why is grief so unimaginative? Is a dream like this just the hope that when someone dies they move on to a new life that wouldn't be wholly unimaginable even if unreachable? Is this a wish to name a place, any place?

In life, my father loved maps, which he traced and retraced and annotated over time, mastering the American freeways with their comings and goings. After he died, I found in his desk a drawer of his map collection, neat stacks in alphabetical order. He was one of those people who had an unerring instinct for refolding maps in the exact way demanded by the creases. The most used one was the map of Georgia, with carefully mended cracks and color-coded, highlighted routes. Like many immigrants, my father was not fond of moving and disliked being lost. After that first year in Augusta, we moved to Savannah, and that was it; he lived there for the rest of his life.

For our weekend trips to Atlanta, we would load up my dad's used silver-turquoise Chevrolet Impala with an ice cooler or two for the six-hour drive and treat ourselves to sushi or dim sum. I especially loved going to sushi because that meant my dad would be in a good mood, and once we found a quality sushi place, we would return to it repeatedly, faithfully. My father would go about cultivating a relationship with the sushi chef. This is how, he said with a wink, we get the freshest fish and whatever specials the chef might be reserving for his own family. Indeed, it was on those trips that I first tasted the unctuous richness of ankimo and live hokkigai so fresh that you could see the muscles twitching.

My dad spoke and wrote impeccable Japanese. Like many others in Taiwan who grew up during the five decades of Japanese occupation, my father might have had negative feelings about the imperial Japanese government, but he loved Japanese food and culture. Of all the languages that he could read—Mandarin, Japanese, English, and a smattering of German (which was required in medical schools back then)—my father was most comfortable in Japanese. At the sushi restaurants, we always sat at the bar, where my father could spend the meal chatting with the chef behind the counter with an easy loquaciousness that I rarely saw in regular life. My mom would bring the chef's wife a saved stack of her *Josei Jishin,* a weekly Japanese women's journal that is still in circulation today. My father liked to make fun of his own Machiavellian wooing of sushi chefs in Atlanta— ("Small fish catches big fish!")—but I could tell he really enjoyed the connection.

I can still retrace our itinerary: In addition to eating, we would visit the Chinese bookstore where my brother bought the latest editions of *Old Master Q* (*Lao Fu Zi*), a Chinese version of *Mad* magazine featuring a quixotic, old-fashioned scholar whose anachronistic ways rendered him both foolish and wise in the modern world. We'd check out the Japanese hardware store and, my personal favorite, the stationery store, where I would be lost in an orgy of papers, envelopes, notebooks, pens, erasers, and pencil boxes. Our last and most important stop was always the grocery store, where we loaded up on fresh Chinese vegetables and other goodies before making the long drive back.

We must have done this trip hundreds of times, yet each time my father would spread out his map on the kitchen table the night before and study his notes. On the trips and during stops, he would take notes in a little booklet: which route shaved off a minute or two, which exit was easier to navigate, which rest stop cleaner and which gas station friendlier. Was it anxiety or the reassurance of mastery (perhaps these are the same) that drove him again and again to refine his instructions to himself? I used to think that this rather compulsive attention to mapping was a symptom of being an immigrant who never wanted to lose his way, not even a little. But then I read about the "Green Book" that informed African American travelers of places where it was safe for them to eat and sleep in the South, and I wondered whether my dad's notions of a more "service friendly" gas station or mini-mart included an element of that anxiety as well. Racial animosity in the American South is primarily reserved for whites against African Americans, but it can erupt against Asians, all the more volatile in its unpredictability. Being prepared for it doesn't mean you'd be hurt less, but you feel at least less exposed.

When my dad first came to the United States in the early 1970s, he was already a practicing surgeon and a research scholar with over sixty published articles to his name. At the Medical College of Georgia in Augusta, he must have been the most overqualified intern ever. He rarely talked about his initial time there by himself, though years later I would learn that he was assigned the on-call shift for every Jewish, Christian, or national holiday that entire first year. Everyone assumed he was the out-sider with no ties. At one point he was advised by a concerned colleague that no white woman would go to a Chinese ob-gyn.

Relocating from Taipei to the American South probably looked like an idiosyncratic move, but, really, any choice would have been a shot in the dark. I remember my parents in our Taipei apartment with a map of the United States in front of them, trying to parse out all the uninforming information in front of them. They were discussing where to go. My father had opportunities in Boston, Massachusetts, and Augusta, Georgia. I often think I would've turned out to be a very different person had we gone to Boston; something about the South, I think, reinforced all the worst lessons of Chinese femininity.

When we finally came to America to join my father a year later, I saw him right away in the crowded airport terminal blurred by pale faces. I ran toward him, yelling, "Pap-pi, Pap-pi!" He halted my headlong plunge with both hands and said, "Stop calling me that. Here it sounds like you're calling a small dog. American kids say 'Dad' or 'Daddy.'" For a second, we looked at each other, strangers.

In that first year, we all had adjustments to make, but our desires were smaller. Against my mother's frugal preference for a one-bedroom apartment, my father splurged, finding us a two-bedroom in a complex called the Sans Souci. Years later in Northern California I would think of the Sans Souci whenever I passed, on the endless El Camino, some prosaic apartment complex with overly ambitious names like the Monticello or the Biltmore. The Sans Souci was a low-slung, two-story apartment building in black-and-brown brick that sat on the famous red soil of Augusta, five miles from the Masters golf course. Each unit came with an identical balcony or, on the ground floor, a concrete patio where people stored their neglected BBQs and plastic lawn chairs. The complex had a playground with three animal spring riders in a small wood chip circle. All my classmates lived in big houses with glistening swimming pools, so my mom was worried about what the kids would do when they came to our place for my birthday party. She fussed about what to feed and how to entertain American children, but we spent that afternoon miming to one another, taking turns riding those laminated animals, and running around the concrete parking lots.

Back then going to McDonald's on Sundays was a big treat, like our strolls afterward through J. M. Fields, a version of Kmart, at the top of National Hill. Even months after our arrival, we still marveled at the sheer number of goods in American stores: everything in every size, open to touching and trying, aisle after brimming aisle. On those weekend outings, we rarely bought anything—"saving" being the mantra then—but we were together.

My father had pre-enrolled my brother and me in a small private school so that we could start school the day after our arrival in Augusta. He picked this school because he had found the principal, a Mrs. Nichols, learned and well traveled. My brother and I were the first nonwhite, not to mention foreign, students in the history of Episcopal Day. We sat through the school days, mostly in incomprehension save for the occasional math equation on the blackboard, and after school, we would go for our English lessons with a private tutor, a Chinese woman who spoke Mandarin. Three days into this, my father overheard the tutor translating English for us in our lesson and promptly dismissed her. He then set about looking for a new ESL teacher; he had two criteria: someone who didn't speak Mandarin and someone without a southern accent. I remember being grumpy: How was I supposed to learn from someone with whom I couldn't even communicate? In hindsight, what I thought was my dad's curt impatience was his instinct that when it comes to acquiring a new language, *immersion*—jumping in at the deep end and being lost—is the way to go.

4. A Form of Patience

It has been sixteen years since my father's death. I always know exactly how long because it was a couple of weeks before my son was born. It physically puts a pain in my chest that, except for that one time, I never dream about my father. Sometimes I would go to bed deliberately thinking about him (I didn't do this often because this could backfire, triggering intense insomnia) in the hope that those thoughts would bleed into my dreams when I fell asleep. I so wanted to *see* his face, even if only in a dream.

Ralph Waldo Emerson famously wrote that grief is shallow. I never understood what that meant, except perhaps that there is no revelatory depth to death; it is such a flat refusal.

I continue to rail against how final death is. Does it have to be so draconian? Sure, I understand that any exchange between the living and the dead would defeat the prime directive of death, whatever that might be, but would it be so terrible, so earth-shattering, if the deceased left a few, indifferent traces of themselves for the living? Just *some* signs. My mother, too, says she rarely dreams about my dad, though she is convinced that it is from a wish to spare her that he doesn't visit. She tells the story of the one time that she cried out to him in the middle of the day and then felt a rush of sudden cool breeze even though she was inside the house. I chalk all that up to magical thinking, but the magic has not worked for me.

I can't tell which came first: my father's death or the awareness of that deep chasm around which I skate. Both feel as if they've been with me forever.

I looked up the duration of "normal grief" in the *Diagnostic and Statistical Manual of Mental Disorders*. The earlier editions state that an expected period of grief in the face of a major loss—

such as the loss of a parent, spouse, or child—could be anywhere from twelve months to two years, after which a patient
might be considered clinically depressed and should seek treatment and medication. But between the third and fifth editions
of the *DSM,* that period of acceptable grief has shortened to
two to five months. I suspect the change has something to do
with pharmaceutical lobby interests, but I can't help but think
how the American narrative of progress leaves little room for
grieving. Every story of loss must have a moral, a useful, saving
grace, and a lesson for a way forward. But what if loss were, as
Emerson said, "shallow," something that you cannot wade into:
an ungiving, ever-absent presence on which our attachment to
and distance from the beloved continually circles?

   In 1917, Freud postulated that there are two kinds of grief: a
normal kind that he called "the work of mourning" and a pathological kind that he named "melancholia." The former is devastating but finite in duration, the ego learning to replace the
lost, beloved object with a new object. Unhealthy grief, on the
other hand, is interminable in nature and refuses substitution. I
always thought there was something brutal in Freud's notion of
healthy mourning, as if we must kill the loved one if we want to
survive ourselves. But twelve years later, in 1929, after suffering
the loss of his own beloved daughter Sophie, Freud wrote to his
friend Ludwig Binswanger that the distinction between healthy
substitution and pathological hanging-on might not be as clear
as he had claimed. In his personal letter, he observed, "No matter what may come to take [the loved one's] place, even should it
fill that place completely, it yet remains something else. And that
is how it should be. It is the only way of perpetuating a love that
we do not want to abandon." In grief, Freud showed himself to
be the consummate melancholic.

In my academic work, I've written much about the nature of racial grief, about how our litigious society is at ease with grievance but not with grief and that it may behoove us to name and *stay with* the ongoing losses created by American racism instead of rushing to *get over* those wounds. A falsely optimistic rhetoric of progress can hide an unwillingness to face the past, especially when that past is not even past. I think Robert Frost got it right: "Grievances are a form of impatience. Griefs are a form of patience."

At the same time, this work and reading about the nature of grief did not prepare me for my father's death. When he called me in California to tell me he had been diagnosed with non-smoker's stage IV lung cancer, I could hardly process what he was saying. Why would a nonsmoker get lung cancer? How many stages are there? How long had he known? Up until then, cancer had not touched our lives. As my brain was trying to unscramble itself, he told me in his calm doctor voice, "They say I have maybe a year if I do nothing, but I know that it is really three to four months. I will do what I can, but I'm not willing to do anything just to squeeze out a few months. I had a good life, and I don't regret anything." I got off the phone, made a flight reservation to Georgia, and then started researching on the computer.

I was afraid he would not try hard enough to live. In the end, after the chemo and radiation, he did agree to do a clinical trial that I found at Johns Hopkins: a brand-new drug named Iressa that at the time had had surprising success in Japan, though the downside was that patients responded very well for the first six to eight months and then less so.

When my mom called to say she had to move my dad into hospice, I didn't know what that meant. Somehow none of my readings about treatments and trials included information about hospice. My mom said it was a hospital with special care and reassured me that he would stabilize and be back home in a few days. My dad made me promise to stay put because I was due to have my baby any day. I had had a miscarriage four months into another pregnancy just a year before. I believed in the lie about hospice because I was ignorant and filled with fear.

The last time I saw my dad was at the Savannah airport a couple of months before he died. I was telling myself I had another visit to plan as I waved to him, leaning on my mom by the security gate. The night before, we had gone to dinner at Hirano's, a good sushi restaurant in Savannah that was a long time coming. Over the years my dad had made friends with the two sushi chef-owners. We walked into a warm, familial welcome. That night, he didn't eat much. On our way out to the parking lot, I slipped my arm into his, hoping he wouldn't pull away. My parents were not demonstrative people. He held my arm to his side with such a tight and long squeeze that he must have known, as I could not allow myself to think, that that would be our last visit.

20

On Aging

1.

I recall being a little girl looking up at my grandmother, who was looking into a mirror on the wall, leaning in, one hand raised to touch her forehead and then one cheek, saying to me or to herself, "That's not me. I see the face out there but inside I don't feel like that old woman at all!" I remember wondering what on earth she meant. Of course she was that old woman in the mirror. Who else would she be?

Now I understand what she meant. Even though those who've known me for years insist that I haven't aged—you know, that Asian ageless thing—there is now a gap between how I look on the outside and how I feel on the inside. Take two pictures of me ten years apart. While you may not discern a crease, there's no doubt that one face is carrying more than the other: a know-ingness that comes with a kind of weight, a slight droop to the eyelids making the eyes smaller, freckles consolidating into discoloration.

There's a deeper chasm going on as well, a growing breach between how I think I ought to feel and what the insides of my body are really doing. Cancer has brought death to my door earlier than expected. Chemo has permanently thinned my hair and wrecked veins and nerves. Other invisible agents are spurring my body to mutiny, making my eyes, throat, and skin so dry that I'm like those proverbial skeletons that archaeologists uncover, the ones that disintegrate into dust the moment the sealed tomb opens, as if the fresh air itself were the curse. Last month I fell down the stairs when my feet went numb. This week I tripped on my own slippers in such a way that I hurtled headlong several feet into the wall with a comic speed that I could feel but not control. My son in the other room said it sounded like someone fell . . . and kept falling. I'm tired of doctors remarking, "Well, this is unexpected. We usually see this in much older patients . . ." I think, deep inside, where no one can see, I am aging rapidly, exponentially, prematurely.

Recently I reread the novel *Mrs. Dalloway* for class. I first read it in high school and then again many times over the years. At the back of my mind I had filed the plot under "a story about an old lady." But this time, to my shock and embarrassment, I noticed that Clarissa Dalloway was fifty-one years old in the novel. That's eight years, almost a decade, younger than I am now. The novel was never about old age but its approach: a becoming, a temporal shift of consciousness, a hinging on the curve downward where hard-earned self-assurance, lifelong loneliness, new and old fragilities start to wedge between the shells that you have gathered over the years.

This coming to aging—the realization that even as you own more and more of yourself, your body is becoming less and less yours—must be one of the great ironies of life. I've started to hate the way the doctors like to use the word *atrophy* when it comes to describing what's happening to my body: there's nerve atrophy, muscle atrophy, joint atrophy, skin atrophy, and so on. They use the word dispassionately, scientifically, the way you would say *diabetes* or *hypertension,* as if they were not actually telling me that my body parts are disintegrating even as we speak. (And should this atrophy be happening so soon and so fast? Shouldn't the warranty last a tad longer?)

When you face the fact that you're never going to be as healthy as you were before, without even taking into account major diseases and no matter how diligently you go to the gym, then you know you are facing true aging. Everything before a serious confrontation with your body is growing up; everything after is aging.

Virginia Woolf describes Mrs. Dalloway this way: "She felt very young; at the same time unspeakably aged. She sliced like a knife through everything; at the same time was outside, looking on." The essayist Jean Améry also talks about aging, or more precisely, the beginning of the knowingness of aging, as this double movement of self-possession and dispossession. He writes this of a woman in front of her mirror: "She perceives her body, which at this stage is present to her as her ego, as a shell, as something external and done to her, and at the same time as something that is actually hers, to which she is more and more reduced and to which she devotes increasing attention." The image of my own interiority turned inside out, as an exposed covering at once fortifying and disconnected, at once owned and imposed, an endowment that is also a debt, haunts me.

Améry will go on to call the aging body "our prison, but also our last shelter."

2.

Even in the couple of years since I started writing these essays, I've seen a precipitous change in my mother from her late seventies to her eighties. Her balance was the first thing to go. In this short period, she fell three times, once seriously fracturing her wrist. While helping her in the bathroom I realized how much weight she had lost. She was already slim. (Women spend their whole lives worrying about their weight; no one tells us that "skinny" is not a good look on old bodies.) She appeared all skin and bones, the way her mother, my grandmother, had looked when she had tried to starve herself to death after a stroke.

That was also the first time I encountered a new aspect of my mom that I wouldn't have predicted: a querulous stubbornness that bordered on being toddler-like. She refused to wear the overnight brace the orthopedist prescribed, even though the doctor told her it was absolutely necessary to protect and keep her wrist stationary. At night I had to talk her into allowing me to secure the cumbersome harness around her waist and then her arm and wrist, struggling with the multiple, elaborate clasps. She resisted my efforts the whole time, and an hour later, when I checked in on her, she would have loosened the contraption until it did no good or somehow managed to get the whole thing off, and then I would have to do it all over again.

She refused to take the pain medication even though her whole body shook like a Parkinson's patient. Her behavior was all so self-sabotaging, so irrational that I couldn't comprehend what was going on with her. She was the daughter, sister, wife, and mother of doctors. She had always obeyed medical authority like the word of God. Yet here she was, refusing to follow the most basic instructions, even at the risk of her own recovery and in the face of great pain.

Then there followed the "button" episode. After much research, I found for her an emergency call service that came in the form of the smallest, simplest, most discreet device. The call button was the size of a domino chip with a single button in the middle. The device came with its own GPS; all she needed to do was wear it and push the button if she were to fall again. She took one look at it and said, "It's too hard to use. I can't learn anything new." I hate her wholesale rejection of learning anything new because I take this refusal to be exactly what's aggravating her cognitive decline. I cajoled, teased, expounded, used her children and grandchildren's peace of mind as leverage, until I lost it and yelled at her to "just do it." To this day I'm paying for a service that I have no idea if she is using.

Looking back on that time, I wonder if her refusal, what I called her "acting up," was her only possible expression of self-assertion at a time when she was losing much of herself. If I found it hard to recognize her, what must she be feeling about herself?

3.

It turns out losing yourself can happen in an instant. One minute I was getting into the car early in the morning to drive to campus, dressed up and mentally braced for a presentation to the university board of trustees, and the next I was waking up in a hospital room. My then eleven-year-old-son was holding my hand with eyes slightly too wide. My husband put his hand on my forehead and told me to stay calm. He answered my flurry of questions and then handed me a yellow legal pad, saying, *Hang on to this while I get the nurse.* I looked down and saw in his handwriting:

1. No, you did not have a stroke. You are having an amnesiac episode.
2. Yes, someone is picking up Shmoopy from her playdate.
3. Yes, the board meeting went well, and you did well. You did not get sick until afterward.
4. Yes, Nassau Hall has been notified that you will not make it to your marshal duties at graduation.
5. I picked you up from school and drove you here when Dirk called and said something was wrong with you.
6. No, this is not a predictor of future Alzheimer's.

He had been answering these questions from me repeatedly for hours. I felt as if I had finally woken from a long sleep, but I had in fact been awake the whole day, physically functioning but disoriented and mentally stuck in a loop. My short-term memory refused to dump into long-term memory, so my reality was stuck in an endlessly repeating present. With each restart, I was told I asked the same questions in pretty much the same order. Worse yet, I apparently told the same (bad) joke each time, "Hey, I'm like the man who mistook his wife for a hat!"

Waiting for my husband to check me out of the hospital, I could hear what sounded like an elderly man next door, yelling at the top of his lungs for the nurse. I must have been on the Lost Your Mind floor. Every time the nurse left, the man would start yelling again. The nurse was as attentive as she could be, but, given her workload, she had to leave him alone in his distress for some periods at a time. She must have learned to harden her heart. I felt sorry for the man even as I found his bellowing maddening. If I were one of his loved ones, what would I need to do, what renunciation necessary, for me to save my own sanity?

It rattled me for months afterward that I could be awake and conscious but *not there.* I canceled international travel for fear that I might end up wandering, lost, in a foreign city. Things I used to do without a second thought became risks that I could not take. It also bothered me how repetitive my version of losing my mind was. Romanticism has imagined madness to be a form of release or freedom from constraints, but I discovered that when I was untethered from time's progress, I was an automaton bound by duties and habits.

The cause of transient global amnesia is often unknown, and the events usually last no more than twenty-four hours. When the patient emerges from the episode, their memory loss often backwashes, so they might not remember what happened several hours before the actual "event." To this day I meet people from that board meeting who chat away at me about a conversation of which I have no memory.

4.

One night on a visit to my mother, I slept six uninterrupted hours through the night. This had not happened to me in years. The next morning I came downstairs and told my mom about my amazing sleep, about how great I felt, how I feel like a new person when I get a decent amount of sleep. She said, "That's wonderful! I'm so glad you had a good night's rest." And then she said, "So, how did you sleep last night?"

My mother is losing her mind. With each repetition of this statement to myself, I am trying to come to grips with it. Sometimes this fact seems incontrovertible; sometimes it feels overstated and rash. She keeps her house and all its matters in pin-order. Her financial records would put most people to shame, her routines are pristine. Yet she cannot remember where she had lunch.

She slices through the day like a knife yet is outside of it.

When one Sunday morning my mother called my brother at six a.m. to say that she could not remember the way to church, a route she had taken every Sunday for more than thirty years, I, back in New Jersey, insisted that she go to see a neurologist. The neurologist diagnosed my mother with early-onset dementia. (*Dementia,* a word not unlike *atrophy:* to the doctor, it is a diagnostic; to the patient and her family, the word resounds with demonic force, a curse of endless torment.) But the test for dementia has its own built-in failures for someone like my mom. I had imagined there would be some sophisticated brain-imaging analysis at the doctor's office. My mother told me that a nurse came in and read a short story to her in rapid English that she could neither fully catch nor hear and then peppered her with questions about the story. My mom is hard of hearing and her loss of English, especially after the prolonged isolation of the pandemic, conspired to make it almost impossible for her to answer most of the questions. *I have never been good at remembering American names,* she told me afterward in frustration over the phone.

Is she in denial, or am I? What is dementia, with all its portent of an ignominious future, and what are normal slippages for an octogenarian?

Améry wrote, "Aging is a form of suffering." I used to think that getting old and getting sick were separate conditions of being, and that it was a matter of the luck of the draw whether or how much they converge. But Améry's words hit me anew. Aging *is itself* an incurable illness, a form of suffering from which there is no hope of recovery.

My mother was the supreme caretaker who did not love me enough. But the newly diminished her cuts me deeper than old wounds.

Aging is a form of suffering. I do not want my mother to suffer.

5.

I think bearing two children in my late thirties and early forties was my body's last Hail Mary. When you are pregnant, people warn you about stupid things like stretch marks as though that is the worst thing that could happen to a woman's body. They don't tell you the real, ugly truths: that pregnancy plays havoc with your hormones and can push you into early menopause, that childbirth can give you chronic hemorrhoids, that the fetuses will suck all the iron out of you so you're a brittle chicken, that there are unforeseeable, weird, lingering after-effects. Six months into my second pregnancy, I developed whole-body hives. Without warning, I would swell into a giant red lobster. The doctor called it idiopathic (i.e., inexplicable) urticaria and said, "It's just hormones" (hormones, like stress, being the black hole into which doctors relegate all things they can't explain). It will go away after the baby comes, she said with confidence. Seventeen years and many dermatologists later, I'm still lobstering.

But I don't really mind these kinds of time-markers on my body. I think of them as my body's vestigial connections to my children.

There are assets to growing old. Mentally speaking, aging, more than madness, can be a form of social freedom for women. When I turned thirty, I thought I could let go of all the nonsense that beset women. When I turned forty, I thought I didn't have to put up with anyone else's shenanigans. When I turned fifty, I thought, *Now I really don't have to take any bullshit from anyone!* (My friend the painter likes to text me weekly inspirational messages, like, "You're the shit!" or "You're too old to give a fuck!") But physically, it has been a downhill ride. Being in "good shape" is now just bare-level maintenance against more rapid decay. I get hurt going to the gym. I get hurt not going to the gym. I don't so much exercise now as practice perpetual rehab.

6.

My mother says she wishes she were dead. She tells me that she is tired of living. She wants to go to sleep and not wake up.

I ask my mother not to dwell on the negative. I entreat her to focus on her extraordinary good fortune: grown children who love her, a beautiful place to live, no money worries. I tell her how proud I am of how well she has lived and managed by herself since my father died. What I don't say is that, deep in my heart, I understand. I get it. Life requires so much *maintenance.* And isn't dying in your sleep what we all wish for: that when the time must come, we would go swiftly and easily? It's not death but suffering and the slow humiliation of degradation that we most dread.

My mother is lonely and bored and unwilling—or has lost the will—to do anything about it. Every time we speak, she tells me how lonely she is, how she cannot wait to see me. Yet she refuses every invitation that I offer. I propose taking her on a cruise to Europe or Japan, places that she once enjoyed. No, she doesn't want to be on a boat or a plane for that long. I offer to fly down to Savannah and fly up with her to our house in New Jersey so she can visit. She says she dreads the eventual good-bye after every visit so she'd rather not.

This reminds me of how through my childhood she had steadfastly refused my pleas to have a dog. You'd think this was because she didn't like dogs or because she was a germaphobe. But I know that growing up in Tainan she had a dog herself, named Robin, after Errol Flynn as Robin Hood and pronounced RŌ-bin, with a long *o*. She told us endless stories of Robin's adventures. Robin, by her account, was an extraordinary dog who practically spoke Taiwanese and understood everything that was said to him. The dog would guard dinner on the hibachi grill just as my grandmother instructed and never so much as think of taking anything. He would sit quietly while my mother practiced the piano. He knew the way to my mom's school and always met her at the gates to walk her home. During the war when the family had to evacuate, my grandmother charged Robin to stay behind and guard the house. When they finally made their way back home, Robin was gone. My mother said Robin would never have left the house voluntarily. He must have been kidnapped, or worse.

My mother said she would never want me to go through the

pain of that kind of loss. When I told my therapist this story years ago, she said, "You mean your mother denied you years of joy with a pet because she was afraid you might suffer a few months of loss?"

7.

I told a small group of my women friends about my secret empathy for my mother's death wish. You can tell your women friends things like this without being morbid, because you've all gone through life-and-body crises of various kinds and because you're sitting together for the moment in a flower-filled garden overlooking the lake, resting in a small pocket of peace and camaraderie. My friends confessed that they, too, have had similar thoughts. Someone suggested that we form a secret assisted-suicide pact. One dictated that she wants to be beautifully dressed in bed with a stash of joints and a bottle of sake when we slip her a bottle of Mickeys. Another wanted us to administer morphine on her favorite beach with Dvořák playing. We laughed as we spun our wishes, because talking this way gave us a little courage, as if we could die with choice and not alone.

8.

These days I'm the one who calls my mom every day. I believe she needs the daily anchor, the small touch-earth bread crumbs that I'm trying to leave. And these days I'm the one trying to keep her on the line. "Is everyone all right?" is the only thing she asks, repeatedly, and when I say yes, she's ready to end the call. It's as if she wants my attention all the time but cannot bear the weight of its imposition.

We no longer have the kind of back-and-forth required for a dialogue. I ask, "Where did D take you out to dinner last night?" She says, "Oh, I just had lunch." I ask, "Have you spoken with your friend Y lately?" She says, "I get everything I need from the Publix." To expand our conversation, I tell her there's a small fox living in my backyard; she says, "Oh, okay, I'll let you go." I can't tell if the problem is her hearing or her memory. We hobble along on these disconnected, piled-on, one-way messages that evaporate into the air.

Let me say it, I'm afraid that my mother will die soon, so much so that this sentence is hard to write. She no longer knows or has any real interest in my life, but she is the touchstone of who I was and am.

9.

The morning after I turned fifty I woke to find the top of my pinky fingers bent inward at the first joint in an angle that was indisputably recognizable: my mother's hands, which I could identify in any anonymous lineup. I've watched these hands wash dishes, mend clothes, brush out my hair. I remember long ago using my whole, small hands to pull and stretch those fingers, at my mom's request, to ease the ache of arthritis.

I don't know why women complain about their necks when it is hands that show age the earliest and the most mercilessly. It may be because hands are our foot soldiers, so to speak, and are the most visible and least pampered, or it could be because the skin on the back of the hands is thin and prone to getting crepey. As a young woman I used to think it unwise of older women to load their fingers down with ostentatious jewelry whose beauty only served to broadcast their owner's withering. Now I think of my mother, in a time before her current fuzziness, holding up the back of her hand like a mirror and saying out loud to her slim, knotty fingers with the incongruously large diamond, "You've done a lifetime's work! I reward you with this pretty thing."

I turn that moment in my mind over and over again. It is as if that memory of my mother talking to her hand were itself a gem, a frozen image of a time when my mother could still comfort herself, when she still had what it took to convert labor and loss into pride and identity.

In truth it is a privilege to witness my mom's aging. I don't take it for granted that both of us are around for this to be possible. What I hadn't anticipated is that I would be aging alongside her with such fidelity. Her eighties are my fifties. I find myself going through much of what my mom complains of: unreliable memory, sleeplessness, parched mouth, inexplicable aches, and confrontation with imminent death. Sometimes a word or a name just won't come to me, and I grow frightened.

In those moments, I think about that character in *One Hundred Years of Solitude* who, fearful of his memory loss, starts to label everything with its name: table, chair, door, bed, fence, chicken, cow, etc. The more anxious he becomes, the more explicit and prolonged his notations: "This is the cow. She must be milked every morning so that she will produce milk, and the milk must be boiled in order to be mixed with coffee to make coffee and milk."

Are these essays my version of these lists, note-trails back to myself when I grow lost? To whom can I turn when I'm cowed by time's sudden pressing? My husband the optimist doesn't want to hear about my dire predictions. I cannot lay this on my children. My mother, with whom I share the same body, is the only one who could understand, but we do not talk of such things. And even if we were that kind of talkers, how could I tell my mother, I fear I am dying, too?

These lines that I memorized since my twenties come at me with new clarity:

> Who, if I cried out, would hear me among the angels'
> hierarchies? And even if one of them pressed me
> suddenly against his heart: I would be consumed
> in that overwhelming existence. For beauty is nothing
> but the beginning of terror, which we are still just able to
>   endure,
> and we are so awed because it serenely disdains
> to annihilate us . . .

I had loved these lines without really understanding them. I had wondered over the years what kind of beauty brings terror. How can one be consumed by something that disdains to annihilate us?

I was too young to grasp where this voice was coming from: on the precipice of a great change, where simply to exist requires gratitude and exacts loneliness in equal measure, where everyday anchors—the duties of care, the getting of daily milk and coffee, the plates and books that we once coveted—detach from their old meanings. Now I see that Rilke was not talking about Death or Art, but about *living,* the kind that we must learn to do on the edge of finitude.

21

Mothering a Son

About three months after my last chemo session, I bought my then fifteen-year-old son a copy of *The Social Amoebae* by John Tyler Bonner. My son had been an avid reader ever since he first learned to read, but from ages three to thirteen, his only other interest seemed to be playing with LEGO bricks. Other kids would put together the predesigned kits. My son would do so and then undo the builds and mix and match and reassemble his own inventions: a whole city, a tree stand where his mini bow-hunting dad sits, a dragon-bird, an imaginary temple fortress with space shuttles. He always seemed able to locate the tiniest exact piece that he needed out of bins of clutter. I wondered if I should be worried that he didn't seem to be exploring new interests. Then one day in middle school, he told me he had joined the Science Bowl. I said okay. A semester later, he came and apologized that he was going to need a ride to Washington DC to get to the National Science Bowl competition. The team had made it all the way to the nationals.

This was before my cancer, when I worked all the time. I felt terribly guilty that I was so busy that my son felt like he had to apologize for asking for a ride to an academic event, but I was glad that he showed an interest in something besides LEGO. Suddenly this kid was turning out to be a huge science nerd, with biology as his major passion. By high school, he and his Science Research Team won $110,000 for their school from some national competition. And just when I labeled him a "science guy," he started bringing artwork home. I was used to seeing little doodles all over the house, sometimes in inopportune places, but to see his chalk drawings and collages and ceramic work took my breath away. Another surprise: he was also turning out to be a good writer. Although or because I was a professor of literature, my children never came to me for writing questions or advice. I get it: too close. It thus startled me when my son won writing awards and accolades from his English teachers. And it's not just school papers; he writes the most lucid, elegant, and mature letters that I have ever seen from someone his age and from someone who has led a largely sheltered life. At sixteen he wrote a letter of protest to the principal on behalf of a classmate who was mistreated by a teacher. The letter was respectful, clear, and powerful. I don't think I would have had the nerve or the tact to have written such a letter at that age.

This is all to say, emerging out of the haze of chemo, I wanted to reach out to my now teenage son with something that addressed all these surprises I was discovering about him. I couldn't talk science with him, but I knew about writing. It occurred to me that I could find models for him of great scientists who were also great wordsmiths. There were the usual suspects like Carl Sagan or Lewis Thomas or Neil deGrasse Tyson, but I was inordinately pleased that I found the Bonner book. I read it first and then proudly presented it to my son at dinner one night.

After dinner, my son went upstairs to his room, as he is wont to do these days . . . no more hanging around the kitchen chatting with Mom. Then I saw the book lying on the kitchen table. Did he simply forget it, or was this his silent way of telling me that he wasn't interested in the book?

I wondered out loud whether I should bring it up to his room and ask him or whether that would be construed as pushing the book on him. My husband said, "Why don't you leave it to me? I'll take it upstairs later and ask him."

Something snapped. Words I could not control tumbled out of my mouth: "Why you? Why do I need you to translate for me with my own son? Why do you have to control everything? Why does everything have to go through you first?"

The truth is, for almost the entire year before that moment, thanks to surgery and chemo, I had to relinquish most of the child care and everything else to my husband. For sixteen years, I had been the primary caretaker of our two children. My husband was a very involved parent, but I was the point person: the one who kept track of doctor appointments, school events, who tended to bodily needs, who volunteered as cafeteria lady, and who drove them to school and picked them up, often in an anxious race against my own work schedule. I did the main grocery shopping (and if you eat fresh food, it's amazing how often you have to go to the store), made the meals, packed the lunches, did the laundry, and listened to my children's breathless stories of what happened to them at school or on the playground. They loved their dad dearly, but I was the person they wanted when they got sleepy or hungry.

No woman really enjoys what the sociologist Arlie Hochs-child in the late 1980s famously called "the second shift." But when I got sick, I wished I was able to do the simplest household tasks. During the "lull" part of the chemo cycle, those respites between the Worst Days and the Next Infusion when I didn't feel like I was dying from poison, I made sure to do what I could to appear *present* and greet the kids when they got home from school. I asked them questions about their days and tried to train my gaze so I looked normal.

A month after my last infusion, I went back to work. I also resumed housework with determination. I cooked from new recipes, cleaned the house, reorganized the pantry, even if I had to do it all rather slowly. It felt like my way of being a contribut-ing member of the family again, my way of showing the kids, *Mama is back!*

Yet it seemed to me that my husband and children, who had handled the crisis so well, just as I had hoped, continued in an unspoken rhythm that excluded me. I emerged from behind the glass wall of chemo to find myself behind another barrier, one that I couldn't quite explain or break through. I sat at dinner lis-tening to conversations with no way of entering them. My fam-ily was talking about movies that I hadn't seen, graphic novels that they shared, characters and strategies of D&D adventures that they had devised. My family was as caring to me as they always were, but it's as if their lives had moved on very quickly and very far in the brief period of my hiatus. I suddenly realized that all my post-chemo-virtue-laboring had accomplished was to turn me into an invisible maid.

When I was my son's age, the big change in my life, other than puberty, was my becoming American, that is, as American as it was possible for a Taiwanese girl in Savannah, Georgia, in the 1970s. My entry into young adulthood merged into my transition from being a foreigner to a semblance of being an American. I was in command of and at ease with my English; I was finding my way into schoolwork, friends, and some nascent versions of a life independent from my family life. It was also around then that my grandparents decided to live with us six months out of the year. My parents turned our guest room into the grandparents' room, which didn't seem weird or intrusive to me. I grew up close to my grandparents. With my grandfather, especially, I spent hours in Tainan following him around the house or sitting in his lap, enjoying treats with him, listening to him tell tales while I unwrapped the thin paper on the cigarette butts in his ashtrays to find the small, cylindrical, cottony filters inside—some burned browned or yellow, some pristinely white—a pastime that my mom abhorred, but my grandfather supported.

In Savannah, my grandparents looked smaller, their movements slower and uncertain in the confines of our guest room. My parents gave them a pretty corner room with four sets of windows, but it still felt cramped compared to my grandparents' compound of a house in Tainan. My grandmother, the more traditional one of the pair, disapproved of much about me: my clothes, my nearsightedness, my beach-darkened skin. My grandfather, who did not know how to drive and so was stuck in our small house in a city he did not know, spent most of his time looking out the window, smoking a pipe, occasionally playing a game of Go with himself. My grandparents occupied a weighty place of respect and deference in our household, but they also moved in the house like ghosts. I had very little to say to them. Even though I had just learned English a couple of years before, it had already become my primary language, outpacing my Mandarin and Taiwanese. It felt like there was suddenly a language barrier between my grandparents and me. They did not understand what I said or my life in my American school. I talked to them, of course: daily greetings and minor quotidian exchanges, *Good morning, please come to dinner, good night, sleep well,* but I had long since ceased to tell them anything.

During my struggle with cancer, my son went from my little boy to a young man towering over me, from a garrulous little child to a quiet young person. This kid who used to talk at me so much that sometimes I wished he would take a breath in between words stopped telling me stories, our exchanges now reduced to the simplest of words. One day I counted the handful of words he said to me that day: *I have to stay after school for clubs, when is dinner ready.* On the rare occasions that he had anything substantial to share, he would turn and talk directly to his dad, as though I weren't there or did not speak English.

Chemo lasted, in my case, seven months. It would take another four months before the neuropathy would dissipate and another four before my white blood cells and neutrophils would return to at least the low end of a normal range. Still, in the scheme of things, a year of nonbeing is not much to pay to stay alive. But, in that year, the world changed drastically—the pandemic, the racial conflicts, the crisis of democracy, the seemingly sudden acceleration of climate change. And my son.

I hadn't realized that the transition from fourteen to fifteen for a boy would be so dramatic. He grew six inches in a year (is that even biologically possible?) and stood well above my head. His voice dropped; his round cheeks grew lean. What used to be full-on hugs that always ended in long snuggles had become this awkward approach: a stilted, momentary, one-shoulder-lean-in affair.

True, he and his dad are often engaged in conversations about things foreign to and of little interest to me: microbes, tardigrades, actinides and radium, dwarf planets, solar winds. I understand that it's to be expected for boys to become father identified or oriented, that he cannot remain *my little boy.* I'm glad that it's his father's turn to be the point person, the one who shares his interests in science and anime and games of all kinds, and the person who helps with calculus and teaches him how to drive. But I can't help but feel that in the relatively short period that I disappeared from my son's life, he left mine.

My bond with my daughter from her infancy through her teen years never faltered; if anything, it deepened over time. I understand girlhood. I understand the transition into womanhood, its ambitions and its reticence. Plus we share so many interests: Jane Austen, art, theater, baking, fashion. She wants to embark on sewing projects together, try to make Totoro-shaped macarons together. She wants to talk about existentialism and Japanese cinema. What do I know of boyhood or emerging manhood or the life cycles of Tetraodontidae?

My unspoken connection with my son as a newborn did not happen right away. Those first few days in the hospital were difficult. It felt like I had just dug myself out of the trenches and then I'd gone and put myself back in square one. Watching my husband leave the hospital with our adorable, sweet, three-year-old baby girl, I was filled with jealous resentment. Why does he get to have the cute happy one who talks and sings, while I'm stuck here pacing the room with an ice bag lodged between my legs while trying to placate a screaming creature?

These modern, progressive California hospitals boast of their state-of-the-art family birth centers where each patient gets a private, full-service natal room, designed to accommodate labor, delivery, recovery, and postpartum care . . . all in one! Essentially, this means that the newborns get to remain in the same room as their mothers, rather than being taken to a nursery in the old-fashioned way. How many thousands of women have fallen for that?

I've never told anyone this because I am deeply ashamed of it, but as I lay in my hospital bed at two, three, then four a.m., having been awake for over forty-eight hours, in pain, helpless against my son's desperate cries because my milk had yet to come in and the nurses wouldn't give me any formula because that might interfere with nursing, it felt like my soul was shattering all round me. And I thought that if I were to fall asleep and someone came in and stole the baby (always one of my worst fears), would I really, really be that upset? Would it be possible to rest my head in silence for a few minutes before the alarm went off?

Looking back, it's clear that I suffered from some form of postpartum depression, but in those dark moments, I wondered why my husband and I had decided to do this.

A couple of days after that dark night, it seemed like a dream. I couldn't believe that was me. I could remember thinking the words, yes, but I could not recall the *feelings* behind them, just as I could not really recollect the physical pains of childbirth even though I intellectually knew I went through them. After the hospital, in our own house, I looked at my son, deep into

his eyes—what makes baby eyes so especially deep and bright?—
and it felt like a palm had closed gently and warmly around my
heart, holding it for me.

After my milk came in, the baby settled down to his new job
of being the Best Baby Ever. Where my daughter had trained
my husband and me in the endless art of the bouncy walk, my
son required only a hug and a kiss and into the crib he went.
You could put him down, tuck him into the pillow wedges, say
good night, rub your thumb between his brows, and he would
gurgle happily and go to sleep, like in some imaginary bedtime
scene.

I found him to be the most *communicative* baby. He had
different cries for different needs: hunger or sleepiness or time
for diaper change, each distinct. I don't know if I was simply a
more experienced mother by then or if it was really him, but
he was just so *clear,* so easy for me to read, and he seemed to
read me equally well. When hungry, he would give a particular
kind of plaintive cry but immediately stopped the moment he
saw me getting ready to nurse him, even when it meant I had
to put him down first. He just waited, as if he understood that
I understood him. Every time he latched on, he would do this
extraordinary thing: take one suckle, release, look up at me,
and smile, as if to say, *Thanks, Mama, this is what I needed,*
before returning to nurse. Even before he could talk or hold
up his own head, he appeared to comprehend what grown-ups
were saying to him. Once my mother put him on the changing table with the rails up and told him to stay put while she
ran upstairs to grab more diapers. She rushed back to find him
calmly waiting on his back, hanging on to his own little raised
feet.

I know these stories will embarrass him now, but I have to write them down, for me, for him. *I am writing against my disappearance.* It has always seemed peculiar to me that human beings cannot remember that period of our lives when we were the most cared for, the most unambivalently loved.

In *The Social Amoebae,* John Tyler Bonner was fascinated by the life cycle of the cellular slime mold because these lowly, brainless amoebae nonetheless participate in a social system. They can recognize their own kind. There's some surface chemistry that allows the amoebae to, in Bonner's words, "recognize kin and adhere more strongly to one another than to the cell of a foreigner." Moreover, these single-cell organisms come together in a coordinated fashion to form multicellular units that gain more mobility and greater chances for thriving. Amoebae of the same family gather to build a chain, called a stem, on top of which more amoebae congregate, creating a large, round ball like a flower, called the fruiting body. At some point this fruiting body breaks off, the amoebae's collective weight making it easier for them to take off and travel by wind to new places. Those that form the stalk get left behind and die; they sacrifice themselves so that their relatives can float away and thrive. Kinship, labor, departure: the bare nodes of biological cycles.

How is it fair that, if we do our jobs right, we teach our kids to walk away from us, toward an unknown future, without looking back?

My son was now seventeen. I had been waiting for him to share with me a copy of his college application essay. I asked. He didn't share it. I didn't push. I wanted him to have the privacy and freedom to write what he wanted. But, at the same time, shouldn't he show me, his mother the professor? Then I found the essay waiting in my Gmail. I see why he hesitated. He wrote about how he had picked himself back up after being broken, like when he crumbled from the stress of my chemo. (What made me think he had escaped unscathed?) In the narcissism of my illness, I had focused on *my* presentation, *my* rehearsal of normality without thinking about how hard my loved ones were doing the same.

I thought I had put on a good front. A good front? I was pale, emaciated, bald, and browless. I shuffled like a person twice my age. I threw up after eating. After I fainted in the kitchen one day, cracking my head open on the kitchen counter (whoever thought *granite* was a good idea in the kitchen?!), I kept thinking how lucky it was that I woke up in time to call my husband home to get me to the ER; otherwise my children would have come home from school to find their mother unconscious or dead in a pool of blood and glass in the kitchen. Thank goodness they were spared from that! What I didn't register was how my absence, those three days in the ICU, offered their own form of terror for my kids. True, all through that period, save for my trips to the hospital, I was home all the time, but I was a ghost on the edge of disappearance. They must have had to practice resilience, normality, hope. They must have had to practice saying good-bye.

I was so relieved that my children weren't small and helpless when the cancer happened that I both drew strength from and overestimated their maturity. And what has maturity to do with life-threatening illness? Cancer makes scared children of us all. Three years after my last chemo session, and I'm still processing the break that cancer cleaved into my life, still cowering under the specter of its presence. Why do I think my son has moved on?

My son grew silent from adolescence. My son grew silent from my cancer.

I don't know how to reach out to him. What is respecting teenage boy privacy; what is me self-alienating myself from my son; what is a mother's role for an almost-grown man who's still a child? I only know how to be with the boy he no longer is.

He must be navigating the new waters of independence and need. These days he drops these little pecks on my head. They are random, casual, throwaways. But I cling to them, these silent messages saying, *Hey, I'm still here.*

As I was reading his college essay, it dawned on me that my son and I were doing the same thing, separately, putting down in our writing what we could not say in person, finding a holding place for our unspoken worries and fears. In which case, let me hurry and write down another memory that would otherwise disappear with me:

At the back of our little Burlingame bungalow, there used to be an area behind the kitchen that served as a transition from the house to the deck and the yard. The space was too small for a breakfast table, so my husband and I put a desk, a file cabinet, and a printer against one side and used the space as my home office. It had no privacy, but the sliding door that led outside allowed the Northern California sun to pour in. In the afternoons, when my son woke from his nap, I would strap him into the BabyBjörn, sing to him, and we'd dance, face-to-face, to Liza Minnelli's rendition of Cole Porter's "Looking at You":

Darling, my life was gray
I wanted to end it
Till that wonderful day
When you came to mend it
And if you'll only stay
Then I'll spend it
Looking at you.

22

Praying

At three a.m. I prayed for my cancer not to come back. *No cancer. No cancer.* I chanted in my head. Then I thought I'd better add no dementia as well, since these are currently my two worst fears. So: *No cancer. No cancer. No dementia. No dementia.* Then I thought I needed to give God something in return, some concession. Would a quick heart attack be acceptable? I couldn't think of that many ways of dying easily. Also, shouldn't I give some time parameters so as not to look greedy, like I'm asking for the impossible? So I said, *Please, please, let me live without cancer or dementia for another ten years*, but I immediately regretted it. Ten . . . too short? What about twenty? Too long? Twenty would take me to eighty. My mom didn't start to lose her mind until eighty, so that would be a good end zone, old enough to have a full life but young enough not to suffer ignominious decay. By that point, I was starting to realize that God had most likely tuned out this petty, unsolicited, one-sided negotiation. And what about my family? I hadn't even gotten to my children, my husband, my mother . . . then there's my brother and his family . . . *Sorry, God, I'm very bad at this.*

That wasn't always the case. When I was a small child, back in

Taiwan, I was known among my relatives for my praying skills. My mother, grandmother, and all my aunts and great-aunts— that is, all the women on my mom's side of the family, which was the only side that I knew—were Christian, either Presbyterian or Catholic to be exact, or as exact as Taiwanese converts under white missionaries could be. My aunts and great-aunts used to request that I say prayers for them, prayers about their bodily ailments or their worries over their children or spouses. They said that God listened first and most readily to the prayers of small, innocent children, so my prayers would be more effective than their own. They would have lists for me when I saw them. Sometimes, if I didn't see them, they would call my mother on the phone to ask her to relay their messages to me. Sometimes, at bedtime, my prayer would run so long because I was diligent about all the requests entrusted to me that my mother would interrupt me and say, let's save some for the next evening, shall we?

I had (still own) a Bible, given to me as a gift when I was a child in Taiwan. It had a black leather cover with gold lettering, pages of delicate, wafer-thin paper that you can almost see through to the characters on the other side. When opened, each page had a barely visible red edge; when closed, those slivers of red collected and pooled, forming a three-sided red sea. I couldn't read all the words in the Bible and didn't understand much of what I could read. But I didn't mind. I loved the smell of the book—crisp and inky—and I loved running my pointer finger up and down the lines, feeling the smoothness of the paper contrasting against the light but distinct depression of each ideogram. I had the feeling that when I touched the Bible like that, without the interference of words, I could reach an unmediated contact with the Holy Spirit. I believed fervently that this tactile contact, more than any written language, gave me the purest connection to being with God. In those moments, I knew I was safe and sheltered by what's good.

As a young person, I didn't suffer the contradiction between my faith and my secular education. I never believed in organized religion anyway; it always felt like an impediment, a distortion of this great spirit in which I believed. When I had to go to church, I tried my best to train my ears to the tenor behind the minister's voice rather than his words, in an effort to reach a deeper meditative state, to *feel* God rather than the veil of human interpretation. In college a dear friend took me to an Easter service at a Greek Orthodox church, and I loved the incense and the long, incomprehensible chanting as all the forms and rituals, precisely because they were empty, allowed me to flood in my own meditation, to escape into my private, numinous communion. I felt I could have my private and personal relationship to God without disrupting my skepticism about established religion.

But as the years went by, it became harder and harder, especially when I saw the hypocrisy, the hate and meanness, the avarice often committed in the name of Christianity. I started feeling allergic to the word *Christians,* just as these days, instead of feeling inspired, I feel a twinge of fear when I see someone waving the American flag. I can no longer trust it as a testament to goodwill or nonpartisan unity, just as the very assumption of a common good or a fundamental civil society seemed to have deteriorated in the past several years.

My children did not grow up with religion per se. My husband and I talked to them about different religions in the world. One year we took them to different churches and synagogues as introductions. We wanted them to understand all the versions of beliefs out there and the choices, but we didn't inculcate them in any one religion, which is to say they grew up with none. So far, my kids appear well adjusted and grounded, full of kindness. And even without a faith in an all-powerful Being, they have a fundamental belief in the *value* of life and of nature. What more could I ask for? Yet I couldn't help wondering whether, in sparing them the baggage of religion, I had also deprived them of the gift of a spiritual haven. When I was small and worried or afraid, I would retreat into my prayers and the comforting feel of those sacred pages under the skin of my finger. My spiritual brailling no longer works for me, but even as an adult, in my darkest moments of fear and anxiety, I have nowhere to turn but my silent pleas to God. What can my children turn to when the world gets too heavy and too overwhelming? To whom do they speak when they cannot talk to us, either because they need privacy or when we are ourselves the source of worry for them?

I had an aunt, a second cousin of my mother's, who was a nun. We didn't see her much. Once every couple of years she would come home for a visit. By home, I mean the house in Taipei that belonged to her aunt, Great-Aunt #4. It was a house in which the women in my family congregated. When my father worked late at the hospital, my mother would pack up my brother and me, and we'd cab over to Great-Aunt #4's house because it was as spacious and open as my great-aunt's hospitality. It was the kind of house where food always seemed miraculously ready and abundant. Although my great-aunt didn't have children of her own, the house was always bustling with life. Her sister, Great-Aunt #5, was always there even though she had her own house, and other aunts, my mom's cousins, could frequently be found there as well.

But it was my aunt the nun, whom I knew the least, who lingered the most in my mind. It seemed to me that she was always coming from some faraway place. I was fascinated by her, her thin face under the wimple, her black wool habit in the heat of Taiwanese humidity, and her calm severity. Much mystery surrounded her. Listening to the adult women in my family, I gathered several contradictory accounts about her: my aunt had heard the voice of God early in her life; she was the victim of a hopeless love affair; she would never marry; she was the bride of God; she wanted to help the poor; she wanted to travel to Rome. It was always incongruous to watch her sitting next to Great-Aunt #4: the latter was senior by several decades but very cosmopolitan, a renowned beauty who still exuded a startling elegance and who laughed easily, while the former with her often-tilted-down head, her silence, and her heavy garb seemed like a large black shadow intent on swallowing up all displays of worldly light or levity.

Between lunch and dinner, my aunt would retreat into her room, not for naps but to pray. I could hear her murmurs through the paper screen doors in my great-aunt's Japanese-style house. My brother and I sometimes knelt outside of her room to try to eavesdrop on what she was saying until we were chased away by adults. And we would hear something else, too: a mute thumping, what sounded like dull blows. When we asked my mother what my aunt was doing in her room, my mom told us that my aunt was whipping herself, that it was an expression of her piety. I felt sick. Could the God who offered me shelter and listened to all my prayers and released my heart when it felt tight be the same God who asked this of his servant? Did her prayers count more than mine because she was willing to hurt herself?

It stole into my head that one's relationship to God might be one of bargain: you cannot get something without losing something in return. This was in direct contrast with what I desperately wanted to believe in, what my elders had taught me, and what I had wholeheartedly believed up to that point: that God was generous and compassionate and capable of taking in all of your concerns, however small, petty, and numerous. Years later, in a different world, I asked a friend of mine, who was a judge for the U.S. Court of Appeals for the Second Circuit, what he thought was the most important quality in a judge. I expected him to say something like impartiality or faithfulness to the law, but instead he said, "Compassion." I was so startled by this that it revealed to me how much I had associated the law with punishment. It's hard not to think of God in the same way, as punitive. And once God becomes punitive, then a whole system of judgment and of just deserts comes into being, and that means a whole system of personal accountability.

One of the most psychically relieving things that my oncologist said to me was that I didn't do anything to incur this illness. Somehow I needed to know that it wasn't my fault for bringing this killer into our lives. I was beating myself up for not having taken better care of myself, for not managing my stress better, for allowing toxic work conflicts to destroy my sense of well-being and poison my body and impact my loved ones. Wasn't I the self-appointed guardian, the vigilant lookout in the family, the one who anticipated and headed off problems? I carried bandages in my wallet. I always had the umbrella or the needed tissue. I stashed a spare towel in the trunk of my car and emergency kits in my basement. It's weird how for all the disasters that I anticipated, cancer, which though traumatic is quite ordinary, did not loom in my consciousness. I hadn't been prepared for it.

A therapist once asked me, "How does being prepared ward off disaster? And does this mean you spend your life looking for trouble when there is none?" Yeah, it kind of does. My glass-is-half-empty mindset ensured—or so I thought somewhere so deep that it cannot even be called thought—that I would not be caught off guard by unforeseen drought. Intellectually I knew I couldn't prevent bad things from happening, but somehow deep inside I believed, hoped, I could at least be prepared, be ready, like a soldier on the battlefield and in doing so, lessen the calamity. "That's no way to live," my therapist said.

Somehow, I had made these pacts with myself that I mistook to be bargains with God. If I didn't allow myself to get complacent and if I anticipated what might be coming, then bad things wouldn't hurt me or mine as much. If I could ward off certain thoughts, then they might influence my material world. I was prone to this kind of magical thinking, which, to be honest, was a form of base superstition. When I read people like Christopher Hitchens, I feel exhilarated and frightened. Exhilarated because his cutting rationality feels like radical freedom to me, freedom from ignorant practice and self-imposed dread. But I feel frightened, too, deep in my heart, fear that he is demolishing my secret last reserve.

Lately I've been witnessing the extent to which fear drives people to unspeakable acts, how people project their fears onto others and seek to control other people, what they read or whom they love, what they do with their bodies: all in the name of religion. I asked my husband why he thinks some people hang on to their beliefs, against all evidence, so tenaciously and so publicly, why they couldn't have private beliefs without needing to push them on others, and how they square this with their own blatant paradoxes or willful selectivity. Why hang on to a God known for his compassion if you want to hold hate in your heart? My husband said it was all about fear, fear made them compartmentalize and blunt the shards of their own contradiction. He thought that what most people feared the most, what made them Christians, was the threat that there would be no afterlife waiting for them.

Had I fallen into the trap of religious thinking after all? Were my fears as craven as those people's? Had I traded in my childhood's pure communion, or whatever this great force was that used to give me strength, for a system of control managed by fear? Has my need for control (the part of me that is drawn to Marie Kondo and hundreds of little drawers stacked in neat rows) overtaken my capacity for the spiritual? I don't think I'm held hostage to the fantasy of an afterlife. I think I won't even know I am dead. There's relief in that true oblivion. But I am afraid of having to say good-bye to loved ones.

I didn't know how much I wanted to live until I was faced with the possibility of having to say good-bye to my children. Even as I'm deeply repulsed by the kind of primitive superstition that held sway over me, I am equally afraid to let go because that would unmoor me completely. Could I let go of my ritualistic thinking and still have some relation to faith? Is faith always and only superstition? How poor is life without some sense of the ineffable? When I am, as surely I will be one day, lost and alone, truly alone, separated from even those who love me the most, sequestered in pain and illness, will I have the courage of that solitude?

My friend who took me so long ago to that Easter service lost all her faith when her church excommunicated her for marrying a Jewish man. She told me that she could no longer believe in a God who punished you for loving someone. When she went through her own battles with cancer, it was before I went through mine. Looking back, although I worried and cried for her, I had no idea, no real sense, of the depth of loss and grief that befell her. I still don't. All cancer patients go through their own specific terrors. I asked her if she prayed anyway during the worst of what she went through. She said no. She never got her faith back. So she didn't pray. But she did do a lot of visualizations, like imagining her healthy cells fighting her cancer cells. And she, for the first and only time in her adult life, kept a journal. My friend's words answered more than I knew how to ask.

Because our body is and is not our own and sometimes needs talking to. ·

Because living and dying can be lonely.

Because this is why I write, in order to sustain an ordinary faith.

Acknowledgments

After decades of working as a scholar, it is both scary and soul-saving to write in a personal voice. A handful of generous strangers acted as readers, editors, and advisors and gave this new writing breathing room: Emily Bernard, Jacob Brogan, Hua Hsu, Kevin Lozano, Jane Kim, and Kristin Lin. Anna Shechtman belongs in a class of her own for being an exquisite editor, ideal reader, and dear friend.

One of the luckiest things that happened to me while I was working on these essays was meeting and then working with Tanya McKinnon, my brilliant agent. Having someone with such mental acuity and emotional wisdom on my side has meant the world to me.

I also had the incredible fortune of working with two editors at Pantheon. First, the legendary Victoria Wilson, whose inimitable style and wisdom (about the craft of writing and everything publishing) served as the guiding spirit through my rewrites and the initial conceptualization of the book. Then came the amazing and delightful Anna Kaufman, whose warmth, wit, and impeccable instincts sustained me through the subsequent stages, which indeed took a village. I must therefore also thank the extended team at Pantheon: Michael Collica, Linda Huang, Andrea

Monagle, Stevie Pannenberg, Vimi Santokhi, Ben Shields, Ciara Tomlinson, and Belinda Yong. Their professionalism, skills, and dedication can be found in every detail of this book.

All writers know the value of having readers who care enough to offer absolute honesty and absolute support, neither one possible without the other. For this incredible gift, I have a group of cherished friends who over the years have shared with me their brilliance, their kindness, their good conspiracy, their laughter, and, most of all, their wonderful selves: Mic Boekelmann, Rachel Bowlby, Susan Buchsbaum, Jason Friedman, Sophie Gee, Saidiya Hartman, Dirk Hartog, Judith Hamera, Bob Hass, Lynn Loo, Sharon Marcus, Anne McClintock, David Miller, Iris Moon, Richard Preston, Michael Wood, Valentina Vavasis, Jill Weiner, and Danielle Wu. Each of these individuals has given me care in unique and myriad ways, through times of joy and sadness. (My friend Bob told me over thirty years ago that what I needed was to find the form of my voice. It feels as if, in all this time, I have been slowly walking toward/alongside these words.)

This book is a work of remembrance, and as such, it enacts my indebtedness to my family, those present and those who have gone before. I grew up with my maternal grandparents as a part of my daily life. When they passed away, a whole world went with them, including a Taiwan that now exists, fragilely, only in my mind. My parents, one gone and one disappearing from herself, animate and haunt these pages. I love them beyond what words can convey, though some of these essays are trying to do exactly that.

To those most intricately bound up with my heart and who remind me every day what it means to *live*—George, Anlin, and young George—not much needs to be said here. This book is for you.

Notes

Preface

x "a skein being produced": Anne Carson, "Candor," *Float* (New York: Alfred A. Knopf, 2016), 4.

x "the unnatural thwarting": Terry Tempest Williams, *When Women Were Birds: Fifty-four Variations in Voice* (New York: Picador/Farrar, Straus and Giroux, 2012), 16.

1. The Monk and the Soldier

5 "In the popular imagination": Cathy Park Hong, *Minor Feelings: An Asian American Reckoning* (New York: One World, 2020), 9.

6 "You can only be Asian": David Xu Borgonjon, "Continental Drift: Notes on 'Asian' Art," *Rhizome,* September 5, 2018, https://rhizome .org.

11 "My body is a haunted house": Jacqui Germain, "Bipolar Is Bored and Renames Itself," *A Poem a Day,* https://apoemaday.tumblr.com.

9. Joan Didion Talks to Marie Kondo
About Packing and Self-Respect

98 "separate peace": Joan Didion, "On Self-Respect" (1961), *Slouching Towards Bethlehem* (New York: Farrar, Straus and Giroux, 2008), 142–48.

104 "Tidying is the act": Marie Kondo, *Spark Joy: An Illustrated Master Class on the Art of Organizing and Tidying Up* (Berkeley: Ten Speed Press, 2016).

108 "Everything about this woman": Jia Tolentino, "Always Be Optimizing," *Trick Mirror: Reflections on Self Delusion* (New York: Random House, 2019), 63–94.

10. "American Girl"

113 "We give death": Djuna Barnes, *Nightwood* (New York: New Directions, 2006), 151.

116 "We were really disturbed": Richard Kluger, *Simple Justice: The History of* Brown v. Board of Education *and Black America's Struggle for Equality* (New York: Vintage Books, 1975), 318.

12. Southern Chinese

139 "passive endurance": Bertrand Russell, *The Problem of China* (1922; London: Routledge, 2021), 163.

141 "Chinese ambassador": Papers from the Chinese Benevolent Society, Georgia Historic Society, Box 1, Folder 0019.

14. Affirmative Action

160 Second, research has documented: Sean F. Reardon et al., "Can Socioeconomic Status Substitute for Race in Affirmative Action College Admissions Policies?: Evidence from a Simulation Model," ETS White Paper, 2015, https://www.ets.org/Media/Research/pdf/reardon_white_paper.pdf.

162 "I needed new plaintiffs": Sandhya Dirks, "Affirmative Action Divided Asian Americans and Other People of Color. Here's How," NPR, July 2, 2023, https://www.npr.org.

165 "A colorblind interpretation": Neil Gotanda, "A Critique of 'Our Constitution Is Color-Blind,'" *Stanford Law Review* 44, no. 1 (November 1991), 2–3n.

168 "Is your individuality": Min Hyoung Song, "Asian American Literature in the Twenty-First Century," *Asian American Literature:*

Rethinking the Canon, a special issue of *The Massachusetts Review* 59, no. 4 (2018): 772.

16. Asian Pessimism

178   "devolving into the Jacobinesque routines": John McWhorter, "When a Racist Joke Does Not Merit Cancellation," *New York Times,* December 20, 2022, https://www.nytimes.com.

181   "Pity the Asian accent": Hong, *Minor Feelings,* 99.

20. On Aging

241   "She felt very young": Virginia Woolf, *Mrs. Dalloway* (1925; New York: Penguin Books, 2020), 8.

241   "She perceives her body": Jean Améry, *On Aging: Revolt and Resignation,* trans. John D. Barlow (Indianapolis: Indiana University Press, 1994), 34–35.

253   "Who, if I cried out": Rainer Maria Rilke, *The Selected Poetry of Rainer Maria Rilke,* trans. Stephen Mitchell (New York: Vintage Books, 1982), 151.

Illustration Credits

Insert Images

Figures 1, 2, 3, 8, and 15: Author photographs

Figures 4, 11, 12, 13, 16, and 17: Screenshots by author

Figure 5: Courtesy of Hulton Archive/Getty Images

Figure 6: Courtesy of Shutterstock

Figure 7: Courtesy of Victor Virgile/Gamma-Rapho/Getty Images

Figure 9: Courtesy of Yoshitomo Nara and Pace Gallery

Figure 10: Courtesy of Lela Lee

Figure 14: Courtesy of the Philadelphia Museum of Art

Figure 18: Courtesy of the Wu family

Figure 19: Courtesy of the Chu family

Interior Images

Pages 41, 48, 52, 94, 97, 142, 211, and 219: Author family album

Page 115: Courtesy of and copyright © The Gordon Parks Foundation

Page 152: Courtesy of the Beinecke Rare Book and Manuscript Library, Yale University

A Note About the Type

This book was set in Adobe Garamond. Designed for the Adobe Corporation by Robert Slimbach, the fonts are based on types first cut by Claude Garamond (ca. 1480–1561).

Composed by North Market Street Graphics,
Lancaster, Pennsylvania

Printed and bound by Berryville Graphics,
Berryville, Virginia

Designed by Michael Collica